ZERO PREP

Activities for All Levels

Ready-to-Go Activities for In-Person and Remote Language Teaching

2nd Edition

by

Laurel Pollard, Natalie Hess, and Michal Marell

Zero Prep Activities for All Levels, Second Edition

Ready-to-Go Activities for In-Person and Remote Language Teaching

Copyright © 2023 by Pro Lingua Learning – Rockville, MD USA

The first edition of this book was originally published by Alta Book Center Publishers, San Francisco, California. This second edition has been revised and redesigned.

Credits:

Editor: **Michael C. Berman**

Cover Art and Book Design: **Laura Guzman Aguilar with Dani Joffré**

Interior Art: **Kathleen Peterson, Laura Guzman Aguilar, and Armin Castellón.**

PO Box 4467

Rockville, MD 20849 USA

Office: 301-424-8900

Orders: 800-888-4741

info@ProLinguaLearning.com

www.ProLinguaLearning.com

ISBN 978-0-86647-578-5

DEDICATIONS

Laurel dedicates this book

To my son Adam, my daughter Geneva, and my granddaughter Sedona: you are the reasons I want to live a long time and keep on growing. What a continuing delight it is to be in the world with you!

To dedicated teachers everywhere who could use a little more free time

Michal dedicates this book

To Jasmine and Ari, who always know how to make me smile

To my mother, who has always been my best friend and favorite teacher

Acknowledgement

To Dr. Natalie Hess, who helped thousands of students and teachers become their best selves, and whose indispensable contributions made this book possible. Her influence continues to spread, a blessing to the world.

CONTENTS

CHAPTER TWO: LISTENING

You'll find more good listening activities in these other chapters:

CHAPTER THREE: SPEAKING

**You'll find more good speaking activities
in these other chapters:**

CHAPTER FOUR: READING

**You'll find more good reading activities
in these other chapters:**

CHAPTER FIVE: WRITING

CHAPTER SIX: VOCABULARY

CHAPTER SEVEN: GRAMMAR

INDEXES OF ACTIVITY FUNCTIONS/TOPICS

INTRODUCTION 1

For Teachers Who Don't Have Time to Read Introductions to New Books

What if you reviewed every activity you ever used or heard of and chose only activities that are the very best ones for language learning?

What if you then selected from that collection only those activities that take no time for the teacher to prepare?

And finally, what if you chose from the remaining collection only those activities which can be delivered both in person and online?

We did that.

Here it is.

Enjoy!

INTRODUCTION 2

The Who, Why, What, and How of Zero Prep

Who is this book for?

- Any teacher who has ever had too much to do and too little time.

- Veteran teachers who want more proven strategies that help students learn — and remember what they've learned.

- New teachers, volunteers, and substitutes who need a repertoire of effective activities fast. These include the strategies and techniques the authors wish we'd had when we were starting to teach. They work. Students learn. You can feel good about your teaching from the start!

This second edition includes 36 new activities and online adaptations for remote teaching.

These activities are suitable for teaching not just English, but any language. For the sake of convenience, the examples are in English.

Content-area teachers in diverse settings use Zero Prep, too! Whatever the subject matter, ALL classrooms use language, and these activities and strategies are at the core of good teaching.

Why did we write this book?

We desperately needed a book like this ourselves. We teachers are conscientious professionals who often work harder than we need to or should. There is no end of need around us, and our profession draws people who feel that being "good" means working ever harder to help everyone — often without enough institutional support. When we feel rushed and tired, we lose some of our awareness, flexibility, and creativity. Students inevitably notice. Enjoyment ebbs. Burnout looms. Students learn less. And all, ironically, because we tried so hard.

Yet the essence of a successful classroom lies in having students do the work while the teacher facilitates. These meticulously curated Zero Prep activities allow the teacher to do just that, and to teach better – more engagingly, inclusively, and energetically – in the process.

A Crucial Distinction: Not "Zero Planning," but "Zero Prep"

We distinguish between **PLANNING** — the vision we have of our students' goals and how to help them get there, and **PREPARATION** — the busy-work we do before, during, and after class.

Here are a few examples of "prep": Do you spend time

- going through readings to find words that may be new to your students?
- preparing comprehension questions?
- creating variations for multi-level classes?
- correcting errors in sets of papers?
- deciding how to engage multiple intelligences?

This collection provides you Zero Prep ways of doing all these tasks and more!

When we incorporate these strategies into our lessons, we spend much less time on the repetitive chores of preparation. The result: planning becomes easier because we have time to relax, observe, reflect, and recover our vision. We find that we're teaching better and enjoying it more!

Highly Adaptable Activities

A unique feature of this book is that it showcases highly adaptable activities. The strategies built into these activities are so effective, so flexible, that we find ourselves using them again and again, varying the content and level but keeping the basic structure of the activity intact. When students have done an activity before, they feel more secure. They can plunge right in, giving all their attention to the task and the language without needing to figure out what they're supposed to do.

Let's use brainstorming as an example of how a teaching routine can be varied.

- Brainstorming can be done with any content.

- The level of difficulty can be altered by changing how much each student is expected to say, or by giving them time to think, draw, or write a brief note before the brainstorm begins.

- A brainstorm may be done with the entire class, or smaller groups may brainstorm, with a representative from each group reporting their results.

Supercharge Your Teaching!

Are you looking for ways to fine-tune classic teaching strategies like brainstorming, mingles, pair work, and small group work? Would you like to see a collection of classic classroom management tips? Could you use some more timesaving strategies across all the language skills?

You will spot some of these in the book. To download the full set, see our free guide *Supercharge Your Teaching* on our website:

www.ProLinguaLearning.com/resources.

What makes this book so easy to use?

The whole point here is to save you time, so we are not going to recommend that you read this book carefully from cover to cover. Instead, use the chapter titles and — even more helpful — the indexes to find the activities you need.

Our chapter titles guide you to activities for the four skills of listening, speaking, reading, and writing, as well as icebreakers, vocabulary, and grammar.

But that's not enough. Too often, we teachers find a book we know will help us, but it stays on the shelf because we don't have time to explore it. We've designed Zero Prep's indexes to take you directly to what you need for TODAY'S class. You'll find, for example, activities that energize your class / calm it down / preview or review material / build classroom community / create opportunities for students to help other students / develop students' pronunciation skills / and so on.

Reading through the indexes at the back is a great way to get started using the book!

We recommend adding one Zero Prep activity at a time to your repertoire. After you've used it three times, you and your students will know whether it suits you. It won't be long before you realize that your teaching life has changed for the better and your students are learning more!

Some Basic Terminology of Remote/Online Teaching

- **Breakout rooms:** These are a way for you to put students in pairs or small groups. You can put specific students into a breakout room, or you can randomly assign students to breakout rooms.

- **Shuffle the breakout rooms:** Move students into new breakout rooms to work with a different partner or group.

- **Main room:** This is the space where the class is all together. You will see an icon for each student. If they have their camera on, you will be able to see their faces.

- **Raised-hand icon:** Students click on this reaction icon to show that they are raising their hand.

- **Poll:** Use a poll to have students answer brief surveys.

- **Discussion board:** When students post on a discussion board, everyone can see what they post. They can also comment on their classmates' posts on the discussion board.

The Two Books in the Zero Prep Series

While this book is helpful at all levels, we recognized the need for a companion book: *Zero Prep Activities for Beginners*. Because the needs of students at the beginning level are unique and require different approaches, we created a book solely devoted to Zero Prep activities for that level. Look for it on the Pro Lingua Learning website or wherever educational books and eBooks are sold.

What Teachers Say about the Zero Prep Approach

Not every activity needs to be zero prep. But teachers all over the world have told us that incorporating these activities into their lessons restores the joy to teaching and gives them more free time to call an old friend, plan a dinner party, relax with a good book, or go for a walk.

Laurel and Natalie, with Michal now on the author team, are delighted to have updated the Zero Prep series for you.

We remain passionate about our own teaching and passionate about you. Our students need us relaxed and creative. So do our families, our friends, and the world. We hope this approach to teaching will be as transformative for you as it has been for us!

Laurel, Michal, and Natalie

Chapter One

Warmups and Icebreakers

Why do we need warmups and icebreakers? They transition students into the target language at the start of class and help students get to know one another, creating a trusting and supportive class environment.

Our students are learning a new set of language rules, a new lexical system, and even a new cultural framework. They may become tense and fearful, just when they should allow themselves to become relaxed risk-takers. These activities help with that! They are non-threatening and fun and will even motivate students to be on time for class!

1.1 WHAT CAN WE HEAR?

Students need to transition from the multiple stimulations of life outside class and get ready to learn. Focusing full attention on one thing at the beginning of class can help! "What Can We Hear?" captures students' interest because they hear more than they thought they could! You can also use it any time you want to rein in the energy level.

LEVEL: Beginning – Advanced

AIMS: Learning vocabulary to describe common sounds, calming the energy level of a class, focusing attention on listening

Procedure:

1. Students listen silently for two minutes, noticing everything they can hear inside the classroom.

2. As a class, students tell what they heard. If they don't have the words they need, they may say it in their native language, imitate it, or use other ways to express it.

3. Classmates confirm if they heard that sound, too, and mention more sounds they heard.

4. Teach vocabulary as it comes up and congratulate students for how much they heard.

> Online: Every student will hear different sounds and can share what they heard.

Variation: On another day – or on the same day – students listen for sounds outside the class.

1.2 EARLY BIRD QUESTIONS

Students often encounter words, idioms, or situations outside class that they don't understand about their target language and its culture. This icebreaker offers them a reason to come to class on time or a bit early.

LEVEL: Beginning – Advanced

AIM: Answering students' real-life questions

Procedure:

1. Early-arriving students write on the board a short note about something they encountered that they don't understand. This might be a single word or a situation.

2. They get help from classmates or the teacher.

3. Move on to your planned lesson.

Note: See also "My Success" (page 8), where students share stories of their successes in using their target language.

This activity works equally well in an online class with no adaptations.

1.3 DANCE PARTY

In many cultures, a party's not a party unless there's dancing! It's easy to bring that energy into our classes, energizing our bodies and waking up our brains. Every culture, and every student, will have their own ways of moving to music, so don't be shy! Students are delighted with whatever moves we make as we join the fun.

You can use Dance Party at the start of class to set a lively tone, or whenever the class seems bored or anxious, or as a reward at the end of class.

LEVEL: Beginning – Advanced
AIMS: Energizing the class, sharing music from various cultures

Procedure:

1. Ask students to find good dance music. It might be from their home culture, the culture of their target language, or any music that makes them feel like dancing.

2. When it's time to have some fun, invite a student to share their music and let the dancing begin!

3. When you've danced enough, go on to your lesson plan – or send everyone out dancing at the end of class.

> This activity works equally well in an online class with no adaptations.

1.4 WHAT I DID LAST WEEKEND

Students get to know one another better as they talk about what they've done recently.

LEVEL: High Beginning – Advanced
AIMS: Practicing past tense, building classroom community

Procedure:

1. From time to time, write this prompt on the board before class: "Last weekend I _____."

2. As students arrive, they approach classmates one at a time and share what they did over the weekend.

3. After some students have shared with a few classmates, volunteers may share something interesting they learned.

4. Stop the activity when it's time to begin your planned lesson.

> This activity works equally well in an online class with no adaptations.

1.5 CLEARING THE DECKS

This activity for sharing good news helps our students get ready to pay attention and shift into the target language. Baltazar may be proud of his new car. Gulnara may have just spoken to her family. In contrast to "How Are You Really," this quick activity gives every student a chance to tell a bit of good news.

 LEVEL: High Beginning – Advanced
AIMS: Eliciting conversation, building classroom community

Procedure:

1. Invite students to think of one good thing in their life that they can share briefly. Since you're using this as an icebreaker, tell students this is not story time and model with a one-sentence example of your own, such as, "My sister is coming for a visit soon!" or "I heard a bird in the night."

2. Occasionally a student may say, "But there's nothing good." Tell them, "I know life is hard sometimes, but that's when it's most important for us to notice what is good." Tell them that the good thing doesn't have to be big; little good things are just fine.

3. Give students a few moments to think. Ask them to look down while they are thinking and then look up at you to show that they are ready. (For more tips on regaining students' attention, see our *Supercharge Your Teaching* resource at ProLinguaLearning.com.)

> Online: Ask students to click on the raise hand icon when they are ready.

4. Put students in small groups to share their bits of good news.

> Online: Put a few students in each breakout room.

5. (Optional) Volunteers may share something they heard from a classmate.

> Online: Students return to the main room before sharing with the class.

1.6 MY ADJECTIVE

This activity allows students to share personal feelings when learning the vocabulary they need about mental states and emotions.

 LEVEL: Intermediate – Advanced
AIMS: Learning adjectives, eliciting conversation, building classroom community

Procedure:

1. Pre-teach a few adjectives such as sleepy, bored, tired, hungry, enthusiastic, happy, worried. Ask students which words they already understand. Offer examples for any words they are less confident about.

Procedure (continued):

2. Ask students to think of an adjective that best describes them at this moment. Choose one yourself and explain why this adjective describes you well at this moment.

3. Students mingle. Speaking with one classmate at a time, they tell one or two classmates their adjective and why it describes them right now.

> Online: Put two or three students in each breakout room. Tell them how much time they have and remind them to share the time equally.

4. (Optional) As a class, students may talk about their adjective or ask a classmate if it is OK to share what they heard.

> Online: Students return to the main room before sharing with the class.

1.7 THE FIRST TIME

This activity allows students to share a special moment in their lives with classmates.

LEVEL: Intermediate – Advanced

AIMS: Eliciting conversation, practicing the past tense, building classroom community

Procedure:

1. Tell students to think of a "first" in their lives. It might be "the first time I met my best friend," "my first day in school," "my first lesson in a new language," "my first time driving a car," or any other "first" that comes to mind.

2. Demonstrate by relating a "first" of your own.

3. Students mingle. Speaking with one classmate at a time, they tell their "first" stories.

> Online: Put two or three students in each breakout room. Tell them how much time they have and remind them to share the time equally.

4. (Optional) As a class, a few students may tell their story or ask a classmate if it is OK to share the story they heard.

> Online: Students return to the main room before sharing with the class.

1.8 PAYING COMPLIMENTS

This activity helps students with the vocabulary of giving and receiving compliments—a feel-good experience for everyone!

LEVEL: Beginning – Intermediate

AIMS: Eliciting conversation, practicing the present tense, learning how to pay and receive compliments, building classroom community

Procedure:

1. Teach students how to pay a compliment in the target language. For example, "I like your shirt" or "Nice haircut!" or "I appreciate you for being so patient with me." Teach the standard response, "Thank you."

2. Coach two student volunteers to demonstrate how the class will pair off to exchange real compliments with each other.

3. Students mingle. Speaking with one classmate at a time, they exchange compliments until you stop the activity. If some students are not engaging much, you may steer other students toward them.

> Online: Put a pair in each breakout room. After a short time, shuffle the breakout rooms.

1.9 HOW ARE YOU REALLY?

This activity accomplishes two worthwhile goals. It is a quick routine for assessing the mood of your class on a particular day. It also helps you decide on the spot what changes you might make to your lesson plan.

"How Are You Really" reveals when a student has particularly bad news or good news. We have had students tell of the birth of a new baby or an unexpected death. Letting the class pay appropriate attention to the student with important news is a far greater priority than getting right into our lesson plan. Even news like "See my new shirt?" or "My brother is coming tonight!" is often enough to keep a student preoccupied. After they share their news with the class, they're ready to learn. Try doing this a couple of times a week, right at the beginning of class. Students love it! It shows them that we are genuinely interested in each of them.

LEVEL: Beginning – Advanced

AIMS: Checking the mood of the class, allowing students to share important news, building classroom community

Procedure:

After you've explained and practiced this with your class the first time, you will need only Step 4, which can be done in a couple of minutes.

1. Ask your students how they are. They will give conventional answers, such as "Fine". Point out that we really don't learn anything from this exchange. When we meet a person we know, we often say, "How are you?" and they answer, "'Fine." It's just like saying, "I see you." "I see you, too." This is nice and it's polite, but tell your students, "When I see you in class, I really want to know how you are."

2. To preserve privacy, be sure to pre-teach polite language functions such as, "Thank you for asking, but I'd rather not say" and "Let's talk after class."

3. Invite students to think about their friends, their school life, their home life, their health, what they had for breakfast, everything. Tell them to put it all together, close their eyes for a moment, and pick a number from 1 to 10 for how they really feel right now. Say, "*One* means you're at home with your head under the covers. *Ten* is the feeling you have when your true love agrees to marry you." Ask them to save number one and number ten for really unusual days. Each student decides on their number, then looks at you to show that they're ready.

4. Quickly ask around the room, "How are you really?" Ask everyone to remember a few classmates' numbers. Each student tells their number by saying, for example, "I'm 7," "I'm 9," "I'm 3." To save time in a large class, just ask all the 1's to raise their hands at the same time, then all the 2's, etc. Invite the class to ask you for your number, too.

> Online: Students can write their number in the chat or say it out loud.

Note: The activity usually ends here if all you want is a quick survey of your students' moods and energy levels. If the numbers are unusually high or low, you can revise your lesson plan on the spot — a simple way to improve our teaching!

When you do this often, you and your class soon recognize that every student tends to have a customary number range. When a student has a different number today, classmates will ask why. Stories erupt, and the class gets real. Assure everyone that they never have to discuss the reason for their number, but that they can if they want to.

Variation: Some students may have information they wish to share with the teacher but not with classmates. To accomplish this, invite students to write a note and give it directly to you.

> Online: Students use direct chat rather than writing a note on paper.

1.10 MY SUCCESS

"Early Bird Questions" (page 2) gives students a chance to get help with something they did NOT understand outside class. In contrast, this quick icebreaker lets students share what they DO understand by telling a success story about how they used their new language outside class. It starts class on a positive note.

LEVEL: Beginning – Advanced

AIM: Boosting motivation by sharing stories about successes in using the target language

Procedure:

1. As they arrive, invite students to write on the board their name and a few words about something they accomplished recently outside class in their target language.

2. As more students arrive, they mingle to tell one another their success stories.

> Online: The teacher writes on the shared screen.

3. You may invite volunteers to tell the whole class their own story or a success story they just heard from a classmate.

Note: For a full exploration of how students can regularly share their successes, see "I'm in Charge of My Own Learning," Chapter 3, page 20.

1.11 SHOW AND TELL

This classic icebreaker helps students get to know one another by talking about personal things they bring to class. Being in a virtual classroom makes this even easier because students may be surrounded by things they care about.

LEVEL: High Beginning – Advanced

AIMS: Speaking about personal possessions, expanding vocabulary, building classroom community

Procedure:

1. Assign one or two students to bring something from home they want to show their classmates. It might be, for example, a photo, an object, something they made, or a short video about where they live.

2. They talk briefly about what they brought.

3. On different days, give other students a chance to "show and tell."

> This activity works equally well in an online class with no adaptations.

1.12 **VIDEO SHOW AND TELL**

Our students may be spending a lot of time online, which can be isolating. This activity lets them create a shared experience by showing their classmates what they've been enjoying online.

LEVEL: High Beginning – Advanced

AIMS: Sparking conversation with video clips chosen by students

Procedure:

1. Ask students to choose a short video they enjoyed. For example, this might be a song or a clip from a podcast or show.

2. From time to time, one or more students share their short video.

3. Allow a little time for students to talk about what they just saw.

> This activity works equally well in an online class with no adaptations.

1.13 **WHAT I LIKE TO EAT**

This activity gives students a chance to talk about their favorite foods.

LEVEL: Beginning – Intermediate

AIMS: Learning food vocabulary, eliciting conversation, practicing the simple present tense, building classroom community

Procedure:

1. Ask students to write the name of their favorite food. Call on a few students to write these on the board and explain any new words to their classmates.

> Online: Write the words on the whiteboard for the students.

2. Tell the class about your favorite food and when you like to eat it. For example, "I like chocolate ice cream, and I eat it every weekend."

3. Students mingle. Speaking with one classmate at a time, they tell one another about their favorite foods and when they like to eat them.

> Online: Put a small group in each breakout room.

4. (Optional) As a class, students tell what they learned about the favorite foods of classmates. For example, Tomoko might say, "Jorge likes turkey, but he eats it only on Thanksgiving."

> Online: Students return to the main room before sharing with the class.

Chapter Two

Listening

Teaching listening has often been neglected because we assume that students' listening abilities develop automatically. However, listening is an important aspect of the communicative process, and it needs to be practiced.

Our students need to understand instructions, announcements, phone messages, TV programs, movies, podcasts, and answers to questions they themselves ask, but they often get discouraged when they don't understand what they hear. The activities in this chapter are carefully designed to help our students develop their listening skills. If we provide them with guided listening practice, we also help them improve their reading, writing, grammar, pronunciation, and intonation skills.

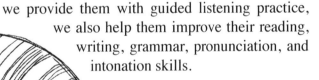

2.1 ANNOUNCEMENTS

This routine turns everyday announcements into challenging listening activities.

LEVEL: Intermediate – Advanced
AIMS: Listening for details, paraphrasing and summarizing orally

Procedure:

1. Tell the class: "You will be with a partner. I am going to announce some information one time. Listen carefully, then talk with your partner about what you heard. When you and your partner think you understand what I said, raise your hands together."

2. Read an announcement. For example, "Our plan for today," or "Your homework will be...," or something from the news. Choose a pace that is challenging but not impossible.

3. Ask students, "How much time do you think you and your partner will need to confirm what I said?" Let the class choose a time limit short enough to energize them.

4. Now put students in pairs. Say: "Ready? Turn to your partner. Go!"

> Online: Put a pair in each breakout room.

5. When a few pairs have their hands up, come back together as a class. Call on a student to retell the announcement. Listeners confirm whether this information is complete and correct. Volunteers add or correct the information.

> Online: Students return to the main room before sharing.

6. Congratulate the tellers.

2.2 SINGING DICTATION

We know it, and brain research confirms it: what we sing, we remember deeply. Here is a way to build up a song line by line for plenty of practice. Even people who think they don't sing enjoy this activity. Not even the teacher needs to sing well!

LEVEL: High Beginning – Advanced
AIMS: Listening to a song, pronouncing lyrics, practicing spelling and grammar

Procedure:

1. Choose a song you know well. If you feel uncomfortable singing, see the note below.

2. Sing the first line. Students sing it back to you together. Work on pronunciation of important sounds as you go along.

3. Sing the first and second lines. Students sing them back.

Procedure (continued):

4. Continue to build up the song in this way.

5. Students write as much as they can remember of the song.

> Online: The students should type the words.

6. Students look at other students' papers and revise their own.

> Online: Put a few students in each breakout room. Students will take turns
> sharing their screen to see each other's work.

7. You or a student writes the song on the board with input from everybody. Final help with grammar and spelling happens here.

> Online: Students return to the main room before this step.

8. Students correct their papers from the board.

9. As a class, sing the song through once more.

Note: If you feel uncomfortable singing, you can play the song, looping back to the start as you build up the song.

2.3 RECONSTRUCT THE STORY

The simplest activities are often the most adaptable and repeatable. Here, students take a few notes as you dictate. Then they help each other re-tell the story.

 LEVEL: High Beginning – Advanced
AIMS: Listening for details, recalling details from a story

Procedure:

1. Tell a story one time. Students listen but do not take notes while you're speaking.

2. Students write down three things they remember from the story.

3. As a class or in small groups, students retell the story.

> Online: Students may retell the story in the main room or in breakout rooms.

Extension (writing option): After the three steps above, each student writes the story as fully as they can. In small groups, they compare their versions and write additions and corrections on their own papers.

Note: To use this activity as a preview, tell a synopsis of the longer story you are about to read.

2.4 STUDENTS IN CHARGE OF LISTENING

This routine shows students that repetition increases comprehension and helps them listen for specific information.

LEVEL: Intermediate – Advanced

AIMS: Listening for details, paraphrasing and summarizing orally

MATERIALS: An audio file to play or story to tell

Procedure:

1. Play an audio file (e.g., part of your listening lab material for the course or a song or video excerpt that you or a student has brought to class). You can also simply tell a story.

2. Ask, "How much did you understand?" Write a couple of percentage numbers on the board, such as 25% or 67%. Each student writes down their own percentage number.

3. With your students, name some types of information they might pay attention to the next time they listen to the same passage. Depending on the content, you might suggest students focus on, for example, reasons, sequences, specific details or types of details, the main idea, names, or numbers.

4. Write a few of these ideas on the board. The class chooses one.

5. Replay the audio file. Ask students to write their new percentage comprehension number. (Their numbers will be going up!)

6. After each listening, students write their new percentage on their paper and the class chooses a new listening task from the board.

7. Repeat until students tell you they've heard the passage enough times to understand it well.

8. Students show and tell their papers. Everyone's comprehension has increased!

> Online: Students hold their comprehension numbers up to the camera or post them in the chat. Ask some students to read their list of percentages to the class.

2.5 CATCH THE TEACHER'S MISTAKES

In this activity, the teacher reads aloud a familiar text, making some intentional mistakes. Students stay alert and interrupt each time they hear a mistake. It's challenging, it's fun, and it turns the tables: for once, the students are correcting the teacher!

LEVEL: Beginning – Advanced

AIMS: Listening for errors in grammar and/or content, using phrases for interrupting

Procedure:

1. Tell students you are going to read aloud a text they are familiar with, and you will be making some mistakes. Their job will be to interrupt you immediately each time you make a mistake.

2. Teach some phrases, from more polite to more bold, for example, "Excuse me," "What was that?", "Hold on a second," and "That's not right!" Put these on the board.

3. Read the text aloud. Make some ridiculous mistakes at first to get things rolling. Try not to pause after your mistakes; you want them to jump right in and interrupt you! Have fun correcting yourself each time, then continue reading.

Note: This activity offers great flexibility making some easily caught mistakes to give everyone a feeling of satisfaction, and some sophisticated mistakes to challenge your advanced learners. Your mistakes can be in either content or in grammar.

> This activity works equally well in an online class with no adaptations.

2.6 PICTURE DICTATION

Using multiple intelligences wakes students up! In this activity, you "dictate" an imaginary picture and students draw what they think you have in mind. Then they go to work, helping each other as they draw, talk, and write about it.

LEVEL: High Beginning – Advanced
AIMS: Listening for details, discussing similarities and differences

Procedure:

1. Dictate an imaginary "picture" to your class. Adjust the dictation to the level of your class. For example, in a high-beginning class it may be something like this:

   "I see a house and some trees and flowers. There is a sun in the sky. There is a sick cat in front of the house. A girl is playing beside the house. There is a road in front of the house."

2. Students listen to the description.

3. Dictate again while the students draw the picture. Encourage them to keep their eyes on their own paper.

4. In pairs, students look at their completed pictures and talk about what is the same and what is different. Repeat at your discretion.

> Online: Put a pair in each breakout room.

5. Dictate the imaginary picture again. Students may or may not make changes to their pictures.

> Online: Students return to the main room for the final dictation.

2.7 DICTOCOMP FOR LISTENING

This activity fosters concentration and encourages attention to detail. For a note about why dictocomps are so valuable, see page 68 in Chapter 5.

LEVEL: High Beginning – Advanced

AIMS: Listening for main ideas and details, creating a writing passage from notes, reviewing vocabulary from a reading

Procedure:

1. Choose any short passage your class has previously read.

2. Put key words on the board. Review their meaning and pronunciation.

3. Read the passage aloud slowly while students listen. (They are not looking at the passage.)

4. Read the passage again at normal speed while students take a few notes about the details they hear.

5. In small groups, students refer to the key words on the board and their notes to rewrite the passage. They try to get it as close to the original as possible. (Each group produces one paper.)

> Online: Put a few students in each breakout room. One student shares their screen, and the others help the student with what to write.

6. A representative from each group reads their passage to the whole class.

> Online: Students return to the main room before sharing with the class.

7. Read the original passage again, if necessary. Each small group corrects their paper as needed.

> Online: Return students to their breakout rooms if a final revision is necessary.

Supercharge Your Teaching!

What's the right moment to bring the class back together after small group work? You'll find classic tips in the "Come Back Together" section of our free guide *Supercharge Your Teaching*, downloadable from ProLinguaLearning.com.

These tips will work particularly well with Step 5 in the above activity.

Chapter Three

Speaking

Learning to speak more fluently, accurately, and appropriately gives students the sense of security and power that they will need in order to communicate effectively in the target language. The activities in this chapter help students to take risks as they acquire language and to enter the world of meaningful oral communication in their new language.

3.1 MY LIFE IN A BAG

Students handle real objects as everyone learns new words. In this lively change of pace, the objects give rise to authentic conversations.

LEVEL: Beginning – Advanced
AIM: Eliciting conversation
MATERIALS: Objects from your home or workplace and a bag or box to collect them in

Procedure:

1. Put several objects from your home or workplace in a bag. They should represent important aspects of your life. Bring the bag to class and put it where everyone can see it. Already, you've created a mystery.

2. When you're ready, pull objects out one by one. You and your students can name them, describe them, discuss why they are important in your life, group them in categories, tell or make up stories about them. . . the possibilities are endless!

3. As new words arise, you and your students may choose words they want to learn.

4. (Optional) Each class period, ask a couple students to bring their "life in a bag" to share with the class. Continue until all students have had a turn.

Note: For a related activity, see "Show and Tell" (Chapter 1, page 8.)

> This activity works equally well in an online class with no adaptations.

3.2 WHO CAN SAY THE MOST?

Students love this simple fluency game. It's energizing because there's a time limit. It's low stress because the teacher doesn't circulate to listen in. Out of the spotlight of your attention, they say more than they thought they could — a real confidence-booster! One more advantage: it gives the teacher a break during class.

LEVEL: Intermediate – Advanced
AIMS: Increasing fluency, listening in order to paraphrase information
MATERIALS: Choose a few short things for students to listen to (an audio file, video clip, dictation) or look at (a picture, chart, mime, video without sound, or short text).

Procedure:

1. Input stage: Tell your class they will be in groups of three to four. The first two or three students will each take a turn speaking. The last student will be the "judge" who decides who said the most.

2. The class listens to or looks at one of the things you chose.

Procedure (continued):

3. Put your students into groups.

> Online: Put a group in each breakout room.

4. Set a timer for short period of time. The first speaker says as much as possible about the input. Reset the timer for each speaker to have their turn. As the judge, the last student will tell them who said the most.

> Online: The judge sets the timer.

Note: Every speaker after the first one has a bit of an advantage because they are adding to what the first speaker said. This gives all students a chance to listen and repeat as well as add their own ideas.

5. Repeat the activity with new input. This time, the roles rotate in each group: a former speaker is now the judge. They repeat Step 4.

> Online: Students return to the main room to listen to or look at the next input.
> Then students return to the same breakout rooms.

6. Continue with new input and rotating judges as long as there is interest.

Adapted from a game created by Forouzan Tavakoli, a teacher at the Defense Language Institute in Monterey, CA. Thank you, Forouzan!

3.3 WHAT I NEED

Whatever you need, if you gather a group of ten people and announce your need, you will probably find help either directly from one of the ten or indirectly from someone they refer you to.

People usually have problems they'd like to solve, and classmates can help. This activity brings students' real concerns into the classroom. As they ask for and receive help, a climate of cohesion, friendliness, and trust develops.

 LEVEL: Intermediate – Advanced

AIMS: Eliciting conversation, solving problems, building classroom community

Procedure:

1. Ask students what they need. If necessary, mention one or two things you think your students might need. Our students, for example, have mentioned these needs:
   - a driver's license
   - a grocery store that sells food from their country
   - a native speaker of their target language to practice with
   - a place to live with cheaper rent
   - a ride to a lumberyard to pick up a piece of plywood to put under a soft mattress
   - a bicycle

Procedure (continued):

2. Students write what they need on a piece of paper. Encourage them to write more than one need.

3. Students read these papers aloud one by one. As classmates listen, they raise their hands if they think they can help. The reader writes down these names.

4. Students mingle. Talking with classmates who might be able to help them, they gather information and make plans. (Students who are idle for a moment simply listen to other students.)

> Online: In the main room, one student at a time mentions what they can do to help the classmate and offers their contact information. These students can get in touch after class.

5. As a class, volunteers tell what help they have found. This is exciting because people often feel that they are alone with their problems. This activity helps dispel that discouragement.

Extensions:

1. In a later lesson, students who have received help write or give short oral presentations about what has happened.

2. Students who have given help write or give oral presentations about what they did. The act of giving help is a fine remedy for students who feel powerless or unimportant. (Don't we all, from time to time?)

3.4 I'M IN CHARGE OF MY OWN LEARNING

This activity helps students take an active role in their learning. On a regular basis, students set and revise learning goals, make choices about strategies they will use, and expand these strategies as they share ideas with classmates. Having students state their specific intentions and ask for peer support can be a powerful motivator!

LEVEL: Intermediate – Advanced

AIMS: Increasing student motivation and sense of purpose

Procedure:

1. Ask students what they want to do in their target language and why. Encourage them to be specific.

2. On a blank paper, each student draws lines to make four columns. They write the following four headings:

What I want to do in my new language	Why I need to do this	What I do now to improve my skill	Other ideas I can try

Procedure (continued):

3. In groups of three or four, students talk about all four columns, filling in their own charts as they go along. Encourage students to "borrow" ideas from each other freely; students often come up with effective strategies that the teacher never thought of!

    Here are two examples from one student's chart:

What I want to do in my new language	Why I need to do this	What I do now to improve my skill	Other things I could do
I want to learn a lot of words. I want to improve my listening.	Because I want to understand movies. Because I can't understand my child's teacher very well when we meet.	I write new words in my notebook with translations. I listen to my teacher as well as I can.	I could use my new words in conversation more often. I could practice using online learning materials. I could also watch a TV show over and over.

> Online: Put three or four students in each breakout room.

4. As a class, volunteers share some good ideas. These can be their own ideas or ones they heard from classmates.

> Online: Students return to the main room.

5. On a regular basis, dedicate class time to small group sharing. Students show their chart to a few classmates, talk about what they've done, change their intentions if they wish, and announce what they plan to do in the coming week. It's easy to break commitments we make to ourselves. We're more likely to act on commitments once we've announced them to others!

> Online: Put three or four students in each breakout room.

6. A few volunteers may tell the class about their successes

> Online: Students return to the main room before sharing.

Writing Extension: Students write notes as the course progresses, describing how they are taking charge of their own learning. These can be posted on a public bulletin board for others in the school to read.

> Online: These can be posted on a discussion board.

 This activity works well before "Real Language for the World Out There" (Activity 3.6).

3.5 FIND SOMEONE WHO

After you teach question formation, use this classic mingle to practice questions, help students get to know one another, and practice writing their classmates' names.

LEVEL: Intermediate – Advanced
AIMS: Eliciting conversation, getting acquainted, practicing question forms
MATERIALS: Pieces of tape for attaching student papers to the wall.

Procedure:

1. Write a short list on the board of things you think your students want to know about each other. Ask students for their ideas and add them to the list. Here is a sample menu to choose from.

    Find someone who ...

    - has more than five brothers and sisters.
    - is a good cook.
    - knows how to use the bus system.
    - thinks that learning a new language is easy.
    - has a car.
    - is worried today.

    - knows how to fix a car.
    - has some good news to share.
    - likes to dance.
    - needs the target language for their work.
    - is married.
    - needs the target language for school.

2. Students copy the list from the board, including the blank spaces under each question.

3. Put question "frames" on the board. For example:
    - "How many _____ do you have?"
    - "Do you have/like/want/know/need _____?"
    - ''Are you _____?"

4. Lead the class in choral practice of the questions they will be asking. For example: "How many brothers and sisters do you have?"

5. Students stand and pair up with other students. Each partner asks the other about only one item. If the answer is "Yes," the asker writes the answerer's name in the blank on the list. Each student thanks the first partner and finds a second one. The activity continues as long as students are actively enjoying it.

> Online: Put a few students in each breakout room. After a short time, shuffle the breakout rooms.

Note: These exchanges should be brief. However, if students find an exchange particularly interesting, they may linger a bit to find out more. For example: "Oh, you're worried today? What about?" "You need this new language for your work? What do you do?"

Procedure (continued):

6. Circulate during the game. If you hear errors in question formation, invite the asker to look at the question frames on the board and try again.

7. As a class, ask students to tell the most interesting thing they learned about a classmate.

> Online: Students return to the main room before sharing.

3.6 REAL LANGUAGE FOR THE WORLD OUT THERE

This activity prepares students to use the target language outside of class. We know that our lessons can go only so far in bridging students from classroom language to real-world language. Even if you are teaching in a country that uses the target language, some students do not use it much outside of class.

The challenges are even greater in settings where your students cannot go out and use the target language. Here are some ideas to maximize students' use of their new language beyond the classroom.

LEVEL: Intermediate – Advanced

AIM: Improving speaking and listening abilities

Procedure:

1. Ask students if they would like to make much faster progress in listening and speaking in the target language without attending extra classes, doing extra homework, or studying more.

2. Tell them that the key is applying their classroom learning in real situations.

3. Ask what they already do to use the target language outside of class. Students might mention listening to conversations in restaurants, watching TV, or asking for directions.

   Put a few of these ideas on the board and brainstorm some more ideas about what they might do.

4. Students come up to the board and write a checkmark next to the three ideas they would most like to do.

> Online: Use a poll. Students indicate the three ideas they would most like to do.

5. Now you know which ideas are the most popular. Choose one or more of these. Generate things students might say in those situations. For example, if many students have checked "pretend to be shopping and ask a clerk for help," you might elicit from students such phrases as:

   "Excuse me, where is/are the _____"

   "Do you have this in another size/color?"

   "Thanks for your help! I think I'll check a couple of other places before making up my mind."

Procedure (continued):

6. Each student chooses one idea for homework. Tell students that they may do this individually or in pairs. If they want a partner, help them find one during class time.

7. Each student gives you a note that looks like this: "I, _____ (name), will _____ (activity) sometime during the next ___ days."

   People are more likely to do something if they have promised someone that they will!

Online: Students post their plan in the chat.

8. In a later class, students report on their results, orally or in writing. The report should include:

   - what they did
   - where they did it
   - how they felt about it
   - what words or phrases they want to remember

Here are some ideas our students have acted on:

1. Go to a museum. Ask questions and chat with people about what you see.

2. If you are teaching EFL, students may go observe classes in schools where your target language is the language of instruction.

3. Go to lectures, poetry readings, club meetings, political speeches, etc.

4. Over and over, watch a TV show, listen to podcasts, and listen to songs.

5. Chat with people who aren't very busy:

   a. at bus stops (After a nice chat with someone waiting for a bus, it's easy to say, "This isn't my bus. Nice talking with you! So long!")
   b. while riding the bus
   c. waiting in lines
   d. in cafeteria-style restaurants
   e. ask for help: pretend to be shopping, ask for directions, etc.

 This activity works well after "I'm in Charge of My Own Learning" (Activity 3.4).

Supercharge Your Teaching!

Do you want a way to brainstorm that makes sure no one is left out? The "Brainstorm" section of our guide *Supercharge Your Teaching* offers just what you're looking for. You can download it free from ProLinguaLearning.com.

These tips work particularly well with Step 3 in the above activity and with other brainstorms throughout your course.

> ### Homework or Quiz Reviews
>
> Want to free yourself from so much grading for more important work? Correcting a set of quizzes or homework papers one by one is not the most valuable use of your time. Brain research shows that instant feedback is far more memorable than feedback students receive later. One final benefit of the next three activities: students learn more when they correct their own work!

3.7 HOMEWORK OR QUIZ REVIEW I: SEEK AND FIND

This and the following two activities will free you from marking most homework and quiz papers and give your students immediate feedback on the work they have done. In "Seek and Find," students circle their errors without correcting them. Then they find classmates who got those items right and talk to them about why.

LEVEL: Beginning – Advanced

AIMS: Learning from classmates why a correct answer is correct, practicing polite disagreement, correcting homework or quizzes

Procedure:

1. Distribute an answer key to an assignment or quiz or simply read out the correct answers.

    > Online: Read out the correct answers or display them.

2. Students check their own quizzes or homework papers, just circling items they got wrong. Explain that they should not write corrections. (The aim is to learn from classmates.)

3. Everyone stands and mingles. Speaking with one classmate at a time, they look for papers that have correct answers for their circled items. When they find a classmate who answered correctly, they discuss why that answer is correct.

    > Online: Put four to six students in each breakout room.

4. When they are satisfied about why this other answer is correct, they move on to look for new partners.

    > Online: Students remain in the same breakout room.

5. When most students are finished, stop the activity.

    > Online Adaptation: Students return to the main room.

Note: This activity works well for assignments that do not need to be formally graded.

3.8 HOMEWORK OR QUIZ REVIEW II: PAIRS DO THE CORRECTING

Students learn more when they correct their own work. Here's a very simple way that can happen. (For more information, see box on page 25).

LEVEL: High Beginning – Advanced

AIMS: Practicing polite disagreement, correcting homework or quizzes, learning from peers

Procedure:

1. In pairs, students compare their answers to a quiz or homework assignment. When they disagree on an answer, they try to persuade each other.

    > Online: Put a few students in each breakout room.

2. If they still do not agree, pairs ask for your help or walk around as a pair to learn other pairs' opinions.

    > Online: Students return to the main room to get more help from the teacher and classmates.

3.9 HOMEWORK OR QUIZ REVIEW III: STAND AND DELIVER

This activity can be quite lively and fun as students vie for the right to be the next reader and vigorously defend their answers. (For more information, see box on page 25).

LEVEL: High Beginning – Advanced

AIMS: Practicing polite disagreement, correcting homework or quizzes, learning from peers

Procedure:

1. One student stands in the front of the room and reads their answers aloud as classmates check their homework or quiz.

    > Online: The student stands in place.

2. Any student who has a different answer calls out, "Wait!"
3. The reader and the challenger defend their answers. Other students may also contribute to this discussion.
4. The student who successfully defends the correct answer wins the right to continue the activity by standing and reading their next answer.

3.10 CONCENTRIC CIRCLE TALK

We use this activity again and again in our classes to build fluency. Without the spotlight of the teacher's attention, students are less self-conscious and speak more freely.

This activity is structured a little differently for in-person vs. online classes.

- In-person classes: Each student speaks to one partner for three minutes, says the same thing to a second partner in two minutes, and then condenses it to just one minute for a third partner.

- Online classes: Each student speaks for three minutes, then listens to their first partner speak for three minutes. Then new pairs form, and each student repeats what they just said, but in just two minutes. Finally, students further condense what they say, speaking to a third partner for one minute each.

Once you have this in mind, the procedures below will work for you. Students often tell us this is their favorite speaking activity — it's both challenging and fun!

LEVEL: High Beginning – Advanced

AIMS: Speaking about a specific topic, listening to classmates, making a story more concise

Procedure:

1. You or the students choose a subject to talk about: a dream, future plans, most frightening experience, etc. (You could also tailor the subject to class content.)

2. Students stand in two concentric circles. Each inner-circle student is facing an outer-circle partner. Give students one minute to think silently about what they will say when it's their turn to speak.

> Online: This activity in online format uses breakout rooms instead of concentric circles. Online variations begin with Step 5.

3. The inner-circle students speak first. Say, "You have three minutes to talk. There's only one rule: Don't stop talking. If you finish early, start over again. If you can't think of the right word, say it a different way. If you don't have ideas, say, 'Ba, ba, ba.' Sooner or later an idea will come to you. But don't stop talking."

4. Tell the listening partners in the outer circle, "Your job is very important. This is not a conversation, so don't ask questions or talk at all. Just lean forward, let your face show that you are very interested, and listen to your partner." For fun, demonstrate your own face of over-the-top fascination.

5. At your signal (clapping hands works well), all inner circle students talk simultaneously for three minutes while their partners listen.

> Online: Put a pair in each breakout room. They should decide who will speak first. Send a message in the chat when it's time to begin speaking.

Procedure (continued):

6. At the end of three minutes, signal for speakers to stop. (Invite listeners to thank their speakers after each phase of this activity.)

> Online: Send a message in the chat when it's time to stop speaking. Students continue with the same partner in the same breakout room for now. This time, the other student speaks for three minutes.

7. Speakers move one place to their right. Now they tell the same thing to their new partners in two minutes.

> Online: Shuffle the breakout rooms. Students will each speak to their new partner for two minutes.

8. They move one place to the right again and tell the same thing to a third partner in one minute. Speakers will have to edit and talk even faster this time!

> Online: Shuffle breakout rooms again. Students will each speak to their new partner for one minute.

9. Only half of the students have spoken so far, so do the whole activity again with the outer circle as speakers. They will rotate to their right to find new partners.

> Online: Skip this step because they have already switched roles.

10. As a class, ask students whether they enjoyed this activity and why. Invite volunteers to tell something they heard from one of their speaking partners.

> Online: Students return to the main room before sharing.

Variation: Start with one minute, then expand the time to two, then three minutes. This allows students to elaborate rather than condense and edit.

3.11 FINISH THE STORY

This activity sparks creativity as students listen carefully and then create original conclusions to a story.

LEVEL: Intermediate – Advanced

AIMS: Creating the conclusion to a story, listening to retell, creating and presenting a story conclusion

Procedure:

1. Begin telling a story. You may choose one you remember, invent one, or read one from a book.

2. Stop at a climactic point. Give students time to think of a conclusion.

3. Pairs tell each other their conclusions.

> Online: Put a pair in each breakout room.

4. Pairs join other groups. Everyone now has a chance to hear other conclusions and retell their conclusion (the second time goes better).

> Online: Combine the breakout rooms so you have at least four students in each room.

5. These groups choose one conclusion for presentation to the whole class.

> Online: Students return to the main room before presenting.

 For writing practice, you may want to follow this with "Writing the End of a Story" (Chapter 5, page 78).

3.12 TWO-MINUTE PRESENTATIONS

Students pre-write, then speak briefly in front of the class. This fluency-builder works best in small classes.

 LEVEL: Intermediate – Advanced

AIMS: Speaking about a specific topic, previewing and reviewing information

Procedure:

1. Assign a high-interest topic to the entire class. Possibilities:
   - A Decision I Have Made
   - My Dream or Hope for the Future
   - What We Can Do to Help Our Planet

2. Give students five minutes to write down some ideas they have on the topic.

3. Each student gets exactly two minutes to talk about the subject in front of the class. Use a timer.

4. After everyone has spoken, students may ask questions. Class discussions often follow.

Acknowledgment: This activity is a variation of one we learned from our creative colleague Kevin Keating.

3.13 CONTINUUMS

This activity helps give your more confident speakers a chance to take the stage. It also engages students with meaningful, even controversial topics.

LEVEL: Intermediate – Advanced

AIMS: Expressing personal opinions, building fluency

Procedure:

1. Write any controversial statement on the board. It may be related to something you have been reading about. Examples:

   - "Watching television is a waste of time."
   - "All murderers deserve to die."
   - "Women should do the cooking and cleaning."
   - "Smokers are irresponsible people."
   - "Lying is as bad as stealing."

2. On another place on the board, draw a horizontal line that represents a continuum. On the left end of the line, write "Agree strongly." On the right end, write "Disagree strongly."

   > Online: Use the poll feature to display these five options: strongly agree, agree, neutral, disagree, strongly disagree.

3. Students write their names along the continuum.

   > Online: Students click one choice.

4. Students mingle. Speaking with one classmate at a time, they defend their positions.

   > Online: Put a few students in each breakout room.

5. As a class, call on a few students to defend their positions.

   > Online: Students return to the main room.

6. As a class, classmates who changed their minds explain why.

Extension (writing option): Students write about their positions.

3.14 ROLE-PLAYS

Students love role plays, especially when they are skillfully introduced. When students do role plays, they feel more free to speak and make mistakes because they put their own identity on hold. "I'm not good at English, but I'm not 'me' right now! I'm a____."

Role playing bridges students from learning in class to using their new language in situations where they need it most. This activity stimulates imagination and provides repeated opportunities to practice conversational strategies.

The activity can also be used for other purposes, such as previewing and reviewing readings or opening discussions about issues of interest.

LEVEL: Intermediate – Advanced

AIMS: Increasing accuracy in speaking, practicing conversation, developing vocabulary, improving pronunciation

Procedure:

In the first six steps, two teams of classmates each get every member ready to speak. After everyone is prepared, the teacher will choose one student in each group to speak.

1. Write on the board an example situation with two roles, such as:

    A. You're in an elevator. You have severe asthma. The sign says: No Smoking. The elevator gets stuck. "B" lights up a cigarette.

    B. You are a heavy smoker. When you are nervous, you need a cigarette. You get on an elevator with a "No smoking" sign. The elevator gets stuck. You light up a cigarette. "A" asks you not to smoke. Defend your need for a cigarette.

2. Designate half of the class as Team A and the other half as Team B.

    > Online: Divide the class in half and put each group into a breakout room.

3. The two teams brainstorm what their speaker might need to say. They might give their character a name, or dream up a past life, family, or personality...anything that helps flesh out their character. Tell them that this conversation could take many directions, so they need to write down many things their character could possibly say. This is not yet a conversation, just a list.

4. Circulate, helping students correct errors. You may also offer useful phrases for politeness (I understand your point, but...) or for disagreement (I don't agree because...)

5. Everyone on the team practices what their character might say. They don't know yet which of them will be chosen to perform.

    > Online: Visit both breakout rooms during Steps 3 through 5.

Procedure (continued):

6. Choose an A and a B. Now that two students know they will be the speakers, they need a little time to get ready. Allow them to practice a few minutes with their teammates.

> Online: Bring students back to the main room after the preparation time is over.

Set the stage for the speakers to perform.

7. (Optional) Arrange the rest of the class in a U shape.

Showtime! The conversation begins.

8. After a short time, signal A and B to come to the front of the room and face each other. Conversation spontaneously breaks out between them. If a speaker gets stuck, they may ask for a prompt from their team.

> Online: A and B speak in the main room. If they get stuck, teammates can send them a suggestion in the chat..

9. When the two speakers finish, they sit down. Volunteers tell what was good and useful about this first conversation. Accept only one or two comments on how this presentation could become even better.

10. Choose another A and B to perform the same situation, building on what happened in the first performance and making it even better (more grammatically correct, more socially realistic, more direct eye contact, louder, or whatever goals you identify).

Variation:

With lower-level students, use simple role plays. Students may memorize dialogs and practice their lines in character. In other words, they may say their lines angrily, happily, sadly, emphatically, doubtfully, etc. depending on the dialog.

Note: Here are two more situations you can use:

- "Bad Grades"

    a. You were lazy this term. Your grades are very low. You present your report card to your parents. Tell them why they should not be upset.

    b. Your child usually gets good grades, but they have just brought you a report card that is terrible! Tell your child everything a parent would say.

- "At the Doctor's"

    a. You stayed home from work because you were in a bad mood. You need a paper from a doctor excusing your absence from work. You go to Richard. He's a doctor and has been your friend for the last twenty years. He has written excuses for you many times before. Tell him what you need and why it is so important.

    b. You are Richard, a doctor. An old friend comes and asks you to write an excuse because they stayed home from work last week to get over a bad mood. Explain to your friend why you won't write them a note.

Acknowledgment: We learned this activity in a workshop given by Mark Rittenberg.

3.15 WHAT ANIMAL AM I?

This activity offers a way for students to talk about themselves from a new angle. The category could be animals, machines, plants, vehicles, or whatever you and your students wish. It's fun!

LEVEL: Intermediate – Advanced

AIMS: Improving fluency, developing vocabulary about a specific category

Procedure:

1. If you've chosen animals as your category, list on the board some of the animals students suggest.

2. Students talk about which animals are most important to them and why.

3. Each student chooses an animal that is most like them.

4. In small groups, students explain why they identify with this animal.

> Online: Put a few students in each breakout room.

5. Each group chooses its most interesting explanation.

6. These chosen students form a panel and present their explanations to the class.

> Online: Students return to the main room before sharing.

Extension (writing option): For homework, students write about their animal. For example, "A dog is always happy to see you, and I am always happy to see my friends." More advanced students will write more.

Variation: To challenge listeners more in the small groups, you may ask a student to present a classmate's explanation instead of their own.

3.16 BACKS TO THE SCREEN

In this information gap activity, pairs take turns speaking and listening about something only one of them can see. Because half of the students are speaking at the same time, you aren't monitoring what they are saying. This frees students up to make mistakes as they reach for fluency.

LEVEL: Intermediate – Advanced

AIMS: Building fluency and vocabulary, describing images

MATERIALS: A video or large picture(s). If these are not available, act out an interesting sequence.

Procedure:

1. Pre-teach key words and phrases that students will need in order to describe what you will show them. Write these on the board.

2. Demonstrate the pair activity with one student as your partner. The student stands or sits with their back to the screen or board. Stand, facing the student. You can see the screen, but the student cannot. Start the video silently (or put up a large picture). Talk non-stop to your student partner about what they cannot see. For example, "I see a yellow balloon going up into the air. It's a toy balloon, I think . . . no, there's something under it, a kind of basket, and it's got a mouse in it!" Continue for a few sentences. Enthusiastically add lots of details and use mime as needed while you tell your partner what you see.

> Online: Play the video silently and do not share your screen.

3. Pair students up for the activity. Position them so that every Student A is facing the screen. Every Student B faces their A partner and cannot see the visuals you'll show. Tell the A students they will talk without stopping, using as much detail as they can. They can repeat information but should not be silent. This might be a good time to go over the words on the board with everyone one last time.

> Online: Put a pair in each breakout room. They can decide who will be Student A, and who will be Student B.

4. Start the silent video or show the first picture. All the A students simultaneously talk to their partners about what they see.

> Online: Post the video or picture on your course site and instruct the A students to view it without sharing their screen. Student B must not view it.

5. At a signal from you, the partners change places and the activity continues without a pause. The video continues (or display a second picture or video.) Partners can switch again, as many times as you choose.

> Online: Signal the students to switch roles. The B students are now viewing the next section of the video or a new picture without sharing their screen. Student A must not view it.

Procedure (continued):

6. End the activity. Students sit down facing you. As a class, students talk about what they saw and what they think about it. If useful new words emerge, write these on the board.

> Online: Students return to the main room before sharing.

7. Ask if they would like to see the whole thing now. Of course, they will! Show the video(s), this time with sound, or show the pictures again.

Extension:

1. For vocabulary practice, students may make vocabulary cards for the most useful new words.

2. For writing practice, students write about what they saw, individually or in groups.

Thanks go to Kevin Keating, one of the most creative teachers we ever worked with.

3.17 I'D RATHER NOT SAY

Sometimes people ask inappropriate questions such as "How old are you?", "Where do you live?", "How much do you make?", "How much do you weigh?", "When are you going to have children?" or "What's your phone number?" Different cultures have different norms for what is appropriate and what is not, so this leads to some lively cross-cultural discussions! Our students need to know how to politely decline to answer questions they don't feel comfortable with.

LEVEL: High Beginning – Advanced
AIM: Practicing how to avoid answering an inappropriate question

Procedure:

1. As a class, talk about examples of inappropriate questions. This varies from culture to culture. Tell about a time when someone asked you a question you didn't want to answer. Write on the board "I'd rather not say" and have the class repeat this response a few times.

2. Volunteer students talk about a time they were asked a question they didn't want to answer. After each example, signal the class to say in unison, "I'd rather not say!"

3. In future classes, you might give students a chance to tell when they used this in a real conversation.

> This activity works equally well in an online class with no adaptations.

3.18 WHAT DID YOU SAY?

When we really want to understand someone, the biggest mistake is to stay quiet, pretending we understand when really, we do not. This activity teaches students how to ask for clarification.

LEVEL: Intermediate – Advanced
AIM: Asking for clarification

Procedure:

1. Pre-teach polite conversational phrases for interrupting a speaker when you do not understand. Post some phrases for the class to see. Tell students that if they don't understand something, they should stop the speaker before their next sentence. Do a lot of choral repetition here so that students become comfortable with phrases like these:

   • Slower, please.

   • Excuse me?

   • Sorry?

   • Could you repeat that last part?

   • What did you say?

   • What was that?

2. In pairs, students take turns telling each other about an experience they had or teaching their partner something they know how to do. The listening partner looks for opportunities to interrupt the speaker to ask for clarification using their new phrases.

   > Online: Put a pair in each breakout room.

3. As a class, students may talk about an experience when they didn't understand a speaker and how they can handle it in the future.

   > Online: Students return to the main room before sharing.

3.19 POLITE CORRECTION

Language learners are often reluctant to correct others. Maybe their boss just criticized them for something they didn't do. Maybe their child's teacher mis-remembered something, or a clerk made a mistake. Practicing the customary phrases for polite correction will help!

LEVEL: Intermediate – Advanced
AIM: Practicing polite correction

Procedure:

1. Pre-teach polite conversational strategies for correcting a speaker when you think they've made a mistake. Post some strategies for the class to see. Do a lot of choral repetition here so that students become very comfortable with phrases like these:

   - No, that's not right.

   - Actually, _____.

   - That's close, but _____.

   - What really happened was _____.

   - No, I said _____.

   - I remember it differently.

   - Are you sure?

2. In pairs, students take turns telling each other about a conversation they had in which someone was mistaken. Together, they practice one or more phrases for polite correction and decide which ones they feel most comfortable using.

   > Online: Put a pair in each breakout room.

3. As a class, students may talk about how they will handle the next time they need to correct someone.

   > Online: Students return to the main room.

Supercharge Your Teaching!

Every class is a multi-level class. Sometimes we have a student who can't do an activity alone. Maybe this student was absent from the previous class, is at a lower level, or didn't understand the instructions. But they need to be included!

Use "Buddy Up: Let the Lower-Level Student Go First," which is included in our free guide *Supercharge Your Teaching*, downloadable from ProLinguaLearning.com.

"Buddy Up" works well with Step 2 in the above activity and with many other activities throughout your course.

3.20 HIGHLIGHTS OF MY LIFE

This is a very successful way to get students talking about their lives. The drawings arouse classmates' interest, and everyone has questions to ask. Students will need time to create their charts when you first do this activity. Later, they will need only about 10 minutes to share their chart with a new partner.

LEVEL: Intermediate – Advanced

AIMS: Helping students get to know each other, practicing questions

Preparation: Create a chart about the stages of your own life so far. Divide it into 3-5 stages. In the first column, write your age ranges from top to bottom. In the second column, make a simple drawing of one important event that happened during each stage of your life. In the third column, give a title to each event. Here is an example from one teacher:

1-18		I get a horse!
19-33		My son is born.
34-52	CRASH!	I have a bad accident

Procedure:

1. On the first day of class, let students guess how old you are, then tell them. Draw your own chart on the board. Let students ask you a few questions about your chart.

    Explain that when they make their own charts, they will each do it differently. Some students will use three sections, some four, some five or more. Ask them to decide how many stages their lives have had so far and to draw and title one very special thing that happened in each stage. They should not give a general name to the stages. For example, "my early life" is too vague. But "getting lost on my first day of school" is a specific memory that will lead to interesting conversations!

2. Now students make their own charts. Give them time to think silently about their lives, decide how many stages they need, choose the events, and fill in their charts.

3. As students finish, pair them up. Invite them to ask questions about their partner's pictures and titles. Invite everyone to learn as much as possible about their partner's life. Circulate, inviting questioners to try again if their questions are not correctly formed. Partners can often help here.

    > Online: Put a pair in each breakout room.

4. Ask students to share something interesting they learned about a classmate.

    > Online: Students return to the main room before sharing.

Extension: Students keep the charts. Repeat steps 3 and 4 in later lessons.

Chapter Four

Reading

Reading is a complex set of skills! Different tasks call for different strategies.

Pre-reading: Think about a time when you read a familiar old story with pleasure or chose a news article because you were familiar with that topic. It's very rewarding to read when you already have a good idea about the content. Yet we often ask our students to perform two different and challenging tasks at the same time: decode words in their new language and absorb meaning. This can be discouraging! Students learn faster and with more pleasure when they read to confirm meaning rather than decipher meaning. The pre-reading activities in this chapter will help!

Post-reading: These activities deepen understanding and can also be used for assessment. We even have two wonderful **in-reading** activities, "Mark the Margins" and "Find a Sentence," which help students read with their minds fully awake.

Extensive Reading: This approach boosts all the other language skills: speaking and listening as well as writing and vocabulary. It doesn't matter what students read — children's books, sports articles, online blogs, fashion magazines, or whatever they're interested in. The more students read on their own for pleasure, the faster they begin to read, and the faster they advance in their new language.

Reading fluency — a student's ability to read sufficiently quickly — is also crucial and too often neglected. "Finger Skim" and "How Far Can You Read in One Minute?", among other activities here, boost fluency.

Students also need strategies for **skimming and scanning**, and for **reading for details, main ideas, or full comprehension**. This chapter has zero-prep, student-centered routines to improve all your students' reading skills.

4.1 ONE-MINUTE GUESSES

Students get creative in this prereading activity! They hear clues about what they are going to read and create mini stories with their guesses about the reading.

LEVEL: Intermediate – Advanced

AIMS: Prereading to make guesses, telling imaginary stories

Procedure:

1. Tell a few details about what students will encounter in their next reading. If the reading is a narrative, for example, you might tell students, "This story has a poor but kind young woman, a handsome prince, a wicked stepmother, and some helpful animals."

2. If the reading is nonfiction, you might say, "This article has a large garbage dump, some poor people, one person with a good idea, new musical instruments, and income for the people."

3. Tell students they will make an imaginary story about the characters before they read. They might

   • think for one minute in silence

   • write key words

4. Students mingle. Speaking with one classmate at a time, they tell their one-minute stories to as many classmates as possible.

   > Online: Put several students in each breakout room. Appoint a leader to make sure each student gets a turn to speak.

5. After the mingle, volunteers tell the class their story or one that they heard.

   > Online: Students return to the main room before sharing.

Note: For a related activity, see "Show and Tell" (Chapter 1, page 8).

Supercharge Your Teaching!

To make "Mingle" activities more effective, see "Touch the Wall and Talk" in our free guide *Supercharge Your Teaching*, downloadable from ProLinguaLearning.com.

4.2 READ, COVER, RE-TELL, REPEAT

The title says it all! Students who thought they were reading with good comprehension are often surprised when they can't re-tell much from the reading. A mysterious thing happens when they read it again: their minds awaken and their reading strategies are activated. They experience real satisfaction after re-reading because they are able to re-tell much more!

Another great advantage to this routine is that every student misunderstands different things, and every student gets immediate feedback. This is differentiated instruction at its finest! Once they're used to doing it in class, encourage students to try it outside class and report back on their results.

LEVEL: Beginning – Advanced

AIM: Awakening comprehension strategies

MATERIALS: A short reading that is not too challenging. Pre-literate students do this with
               pictures rather than print.

Procedure:

1. Students silently read a sentence or short passage.

2. Stop them after a short time.

3. Direct them to re-tell what they remember. You have two options:

    a. Individually, students retell to themselves what they just read. If they can't hear their own voice among the other voices, have them cup their hands behind their ears with their hands open to the front. Try this yourself; it really works!

    b. In pairs, students go back and forth, re-telling each other what they can remember from what they all just read.

    > Online: Put a pair in each breakout room.

4. Students look at the same passage again. As they re-read,

    a. individuals notice what they got right and wrong,

    b. or pairs point out things to each other as they re-read: "See, I got that part right!" "Oh, we forgot this!"

5. Ask students what they noticed about this activity. Tell them they can read, cover, re-tell, and repeat any time to boost their comprehension no matter what they are reading or listening to.

    > Online: Students return to the main room before sharing.

Variation: Alternatively, you can use a listening passage, chart, or picture.

Extensions:

1. Students may re-tell the same passage again, then re-read it a third time. This time, they REALLY understand it! You and your students will decide how times to read and re-tell the passage.

Extensions (continued):

2. Students finish one text and then do another. Here are some examples:

   a. They might "Read / Cover / Re-tell / Re-read" the first sentence in a paragraph. Then they "Read / Cover / Re-tell / Re-read" the last sentence in that paragraph. They'll have a very good grasp of the main ideas before they read the whole paragraph!

   b. They might "Read / Cover / Re-tell / Re-read" a paragraph from a content area chapter. Then they look at the accompanying chart and re-tell that. They'll be teaching and learning the academic concepts on their own.

4.3 TELLING BACK AND FORTH

In this pair activity, students read two different short texts, then put them away before telling each other what they remember. Students have to read carefully, paraphrase, and listen carefully in order to tell their partner what they just heard.

Every student will remember things differently. When they finally read the full text together, you'll be delighted to notice that ALL of them are getting immediate, personalized feedback about correctness. This is individualized instruction at its finest, designed right into the activity!

LEVEL: Intermediate – Advanced

AIMS: Reading short texts, repeating information to classmates to confirm understanding, writing summaries

MATERIALS: Two short texts with vocabulary students are familiar with

Procedure:

1. Tell students that they will be working in pairs to teach their partner a short text.

2. Put students in pairs. Every A student silently reads the A text; every B student silently reads the B text.

   > Online: Divide your class into A's and B's. Send all of the A's one private message and the B's another private message. This can be done via email or in the chat. Then put a pair in each breakout room with an A and a B in each room.

3. Students put their texts away. They must not look at them during Steps 4 and 5.

4. Now the fun begins! Every A student tells their B partner what they just read. "My reading says…."

5. The pairs talk about A's text: Each B repeats to A everything they just heard: "Oh, so what you read says__." A repeats any information B misunderstood or forgot: "Almost right, but _____." B tells the information again until A is satisfied.

6. The payoff: Both students look at A's text to discover together whether their retelling was complete and correct. Direct them by saying, "Four eyes on one paper." Students are excited to see what they got right, and if they discover mistakes, they get immediate feedback.

Procedure (continued):

7. When most pairs are finished looking at A's text together, they switch roles. Now it is B's turn to do Steps 4-6: Give B students a moment to review their text. Then they tell their A partner what they just read. A repeats this. B offers corrections. Together, they look at B's text.

> Online Adaptation: In the chat, send a message to all the breakout rooms telling students to switch roles.

Extension (writing option): If some pairs finish working in both directions early, they put away their texts again and individually write in their own words what they understood of both texts. They compare their paraphrases with their partner.

4.4 STAND BY YOUR WORD

We all know it is important to pre-teach vocabulary before a reading. However, why pre-teach words that students may already know? This activity puts students in charge of pre-teaching words they already feel confident about.

LEVEL: High Beginning – Advanced

AIMS: Reviewing words, practicing pronunciation, students helping classmates

Procedure:

1. Before a reading, write on the board some words that may be new to students.

2. Read the words aloud; the class repeats them.

3. Volunteers choose a word they know very well and write it large on a piece of paper.

4. These students stand along the wall holding their paper in front of them. Classmates circulate, visiting words they don't feel confident about. The students along the wall use their words in a sentence and add any other information they wish in order to explain the meaning.

> Online: Put three to five students in each breakout room. Students can hold their words up to the camera or type them in the chat.

5. Students move freely, standing by the wall to teach a word or circulating to learn from a classmate, as they wish.

> Online: After a short time, shuffle the breakout rooms.

6. Pre-teach any remaining words. Now your students are ready for the reading!

4.5 FINGER SKIM

This activity encourages readers to take risks and read faster. It is game-like and communal: even though students are doing something that is quite challenging, anxiety doesn't creep in.

LEVEL: Intermediate – Advanced
AIM: Increasing students' reading speed

Procedure:

1. Tell students, "Sometimes we read to understand completely. But other times we look at a reading to decide whether it is interesting or important enough to read. Or we look at a reading to get a quick, general idea about it. Let's practice taking a quick look at a reading."

2. Choose a one-page reading that all students have access to.

    > Online: Display the one-page reading.

3. Demonstrate "finger drag": position your finger in the middle of the first line of text and move your finger straight down the middle of the text for fifteen seconds as your eyes follow your finger. (A student can time you.) Then put away the reading.

    > Online: Model the "quick skim" on a screen using the cursor instead of your finger. Then stop sharing your screen.

4. Tell students, "I didn't look at all the words. I looked only at the middle of the page. My eyes followed my finger. But I can remember some things!" Tell them several words you saw. Keep this very simple, so they don't feel pressured by your example.

5. Students look at a new one-page reading.

    > Online: Display a new reading.

6. When you call, "Begin!" students do a "finger drag" down the page. After fifteen seconds, call, "Stop!" Students put their reading away.

    > Online: Students do a "cursor drag."

7. As a class, students pool their knowledge, recalling everything they can. It usually surprises them that they caught not just single words (as you did, in your demonstration) but whole phrases and even general ideas. If they are collectively getting about half the meaning, you have found the right level. If not, adjust the length or the difficulty level of the passage next time.

Note: Eventually, students realize that skimming is not only a game, but a very useful technique that they can apply to many reading tasks.

Acknowledgment: We wish to thank Laurel's sister, Dr. Darcie Smith-Smiley, a creative elementary school teacher in Nevada, for this useful activity.

An Introduction to Jigsaw Activities

In a jigsaw puzzle, there are many pieces. When you put them together, you see the whole picture. In jigsaw activities, students are responsible for different pieces of information and must share them to understand a reading or listening text.

Jigsaw activities are great for multi-level classes because you can give easier bits to your lower-level students. Jigsaw allows more-advanced students to be teachers and gives less-advanced students the opportunity to shine as experts on what they have prepared.

Jigsaws are incredibly flexible, as you will see in the three activities that follow. You can use various forms of Jigsaws as, for example, pre-reading activities to increase interest, post-reading activities to review a reading, and activities with many other purposes.

4.6 CLASSIC JIGSAW

Here it is: The basic form from which our other Jigsaws are derived.

LEVEL: Beginning – Advanced

AIMS: Reading to teach other classmates, discussing the content of a specific or assigned reading

SETUP: Divide a text into three or four equal sections.

Procedure:

1.   Pre-teach any words your students may not know.

2.   Divide class into three or four "preparation" groups. Give each group a section to read. (Assign a shorter or easier section to a group that is less advanced.)

3.   Tell them that before these groups disperse, everyone in each group will become an "expert" on their section. It will be every student's job to explain their section to classmates who have not read it.

> Online: Put a group in each breakout room.

4.   Assign each "preparation" group their section to read silently. Each student raises their hand when they have finished their silent reading. Fast readers will wait a few moments.

> Online: Students use raised hand icon to show that they have finished reading.

5.   Group members talk about the content of their reading section, and each student writes a few key words to help them remember what they just learned.

Procedure (continued):

6. Re-group students into new "expert" groups. Each group needs one or more students from each of the original groups.

> Online: Shuffle the breakout rooms so that each new room has at least one member from every one of the preparation groups. (You may have more groups with fewer students in each at this point).

7. Each expert teaches their material to the classmates who have not read it.

8. Finish with a class discussion.

> Online: Students return to the main room for the class discussion.

4.7 PARAGRAPH JIGSAW

This excellent pre-reading activity takes time but generates a great deal of language! Use it for longer readings.

LEVEL: Advanced

AIM: Reading to share information, discussing reading content

Procedure:

Demonstration Stage:

1. Dictate the first and last sentences of Paragraph One of a new reading.

2. In small groups, students guess what the paragraph may be about. A secretary in each group takes notes.

> Online: Put a small group in each breakout room.

3. A spokesperson from each group reports to the whole class on their guesses.

> Online: Students return to the main room before sharing.

Now the Jigsaw begins:

4. Divide the class into "preparation" groups, one for each of the remaining paragraphs.

5. Dictate the first and last sentences of one paragraph to each group. Each group is now responsible for a new paragraph.

> Online: Put each group in a breakout room. Then visit each group to read the sentences.

6. Each group speculates on the content of their new paragraph. Each student writes a few key words as they listen to the people in their group.

Procedure (continued):

7. Re-group students into new "expert" groups. Each group needs one or more students from each of the original groups.

> Online: Shuffle the breakout rooms so that each new room has at least one member from every one of the preparation groups. (You may have more groups with fewer students in each at this point.)

8. A spokesperson from each group reports on the group's opinion of what the entire article is about.

> Online: Students return to the main room before sharing.

> **Note**: This step can be very interesting. Although students were given the same sentences and shared their information in their "preparation" group, the speculations of the "expert" groups will be quite varied!

9. Give the entire reading passage with a summary assignment for homework or as silent reading in class.

4.8 QUESTION JIGSAW

In this thorough pre-reading activity, students don't move from one group to another as is usual with jigsaws. Instead, they write questions about their section of the reading and pass them to another group to answer.

LEVEL: Intermediate – Advanced

AIMS: Reading to generate questions, discussing reading content with classmates, improving pronunciation

SETUP: Divide a reading passage into a few sections. Cut these up to distribute to groups.

> Online: Post folders on your course site with these sections.

Procedure:

1. Assign different sections of the reading to small groups. In these groups, students read their assigned section. They take turns reading each sentence aloud.

> Online: Put a group in each breakout room. Each group opens the folder with their assigned section of the reading. It is important that students not look at other sections of the reading until Step 6.

2. Together, they formulate 1-3 questions that are answered in their section. A secretary writes these questions. Circulate, checking for correct question formation.

Procedure (continued):

3. Students pass their questions to a group that read a different section. The receiving group looks at the section of the reading that answers these questions. A secretary writes their answers. (If you have enough time, students pass their questions to more groups).

> Online: Students post their questions on a discussion board. Each group chooses a set of questions to answer. Your faster groups will have time to answer more than one set.

4. At this point, everybody has heard information about at least two sections of the reading. A spokesperson from each group reports a set of questions and answers to the entire class.

> Online: Students return to the main room before sharing.

5. The class speculates on the content of the entire reading. They may make up a title.

6. Assign the entire reading for homework.

4.9 READERS OUTSIDE THE ROOM

One good strategy in multi-level classes is to provide different tasks for different students. In this clever reading/speaking activity, slower readers stay in the room to practice asking questions you have given them about the reading. This is an excellent pre-reading activity. At the same time, faster readers go outside the room to read the passage. Later, when students pair up to ask and answer the questions, everyone learns the material — and everyone succeeds at a task they can do well!

LEVEL: Intermediate – Advanced

AIMS: Improving reading comprehension, differentiating instruction in a multi-level class

MATERIALS: Choose a new reading passage. Make copies of a list of questions about the reading for half of your students.

SETUP: In advance, decide privately which half of your students are slower readers and which half are your more proficient readers.

Procedure:

1. Give half of your class, the faster readers, a new reading. Send them outside the room (or into a corner) to read it silently.

> Online: Put each reader in their own breakout room. They read the passage silently. Email them a copy of the reading so that the other group cannot see it.

Procedure (continued):

2. While the students outside the class are reading, give a list of questions about the reading to your slower readers. They practice reading the questions aloud. You have two options here:

    -   If the reading is short, give each of these students a copy of the questions.
    -   If the reading is longer, give only one student the list of questions. This student dictates the questions for the other students to write down. This option gives the readers outside the class enough time to finish reading.

    > Online: Keep the students with the questions in the main room to practice. Email them a copy of the questions so that the other group cannot see it.

3. Bring the readers back into the room. They pair up with a classmate who has practiced the questions. Each questioner asks the questions they have practiced. They get answers from their partner who did the reading.

    > Online: Pair up a reader and a student with the questions in each breakout room.

Important Note: During Step 3, instruct students to keep both the question paper and the reading behind their backs. Tell them they may bring their papers out and glance at them when they need to, but they have to put the paper behind their back again before they speak. It's amazing! Their brains get activated, and they process the material more deeply.

Acknowledgement: We learned this activity from Kevin Keating. Thanks, Kevin!

4.10 HOW FAR CAN YOU READ IN ONE MINUTE?

Fluency is as important for readers as it is for speakers. This powerful game will help your students read faster without stopping for every little thing. They are often surprised by how much they understand when they read faster. This activity is great for multi-level classes because every student works at their own pace.

LEVEL: High Beginning – Advanced

AIMS: Improving reading fluency, escaping perfectionism, learning that repeated reading boosts comprehension.

Procedure:

1. Provide a reading text. Tell students that in this game, they will start reading when they hear your signal. The moment they hear your signal again, they must STOP — even if they're in the middle of a word — and hide the reading. Depending on the level of your class, give them a short time — thirty seconds, or as much as one minute.

2. Repeat this several times with the same passage. Each time, remind students to start again from the beginning of the reading. With each repetition, students read farther and comprehend more.

3. Ask students what they think about this activity. Praise them for reading fast and point out that we often understand more when we don't stop for every word. Point out that when they don't understand something they read, it's helpful to read it again!

4.11 WHAT WE ALREADY KNOW

This activity demonstrates respect for students' knowledge and awakens their curiosity before they read.

LEVEL: High Beginning – Advanced

AIMS: Discussing background knowledge, developing pre-reading skills

Procedure:

1. Wake up students' background knowledge by asking, "What do we already know about _____ (the subject of their next reading)?"

2. As students offer ideas, list them on the board under three categories:

   • things we know

   • things we think are true

   • questions we have about this subject

3. Students read the article in class or for homework. As they read, they naturally notice whether their prereading ideas are confirmed (or not confirmed!).

4. (optional) Look back at the prereading ideas after students finish reading. This can happen in pairs, in groups, or as a whole class.

> Online: Put students in breakout rooms if you want them to work in pairs or groups.

4.12 PREDICTING FROM THE CLUES

Many readings offer clues about their content along with the text. This activity helps students get in the habit of noticing these before they read.

LEVEL: High Beginning – Advanced

AIM: Prereading to make predictions

MATERIALS: A reading with a title, headings, pictures, or other clues about the content

Procedure:

1. Show a reading passage. Call students' attention to the title. Ask them to notice other clues to what they are about to read (e.g., pictures, captions, headings, charts, or words in bold type).

2. With books closed, students discuss in small groups what they think this reading might be about.

> Online: Put a few students in each breakout room. Students should keep the reading out of view.

Procedure (continued):

3. Groups report their ideas to the whole class. Note some of these on the board.

> Online: Students return to the main room before sharing.

4. Students read the passage.

5. As a class, discuss how close their predictions were.

4.13 STUDENT-MADE TESTS

When they create their own test items, students have a chance to review the content and remember what they have learned.

LEVEL: Intermediate – Advanced
AIM: Reviewing material

Procedure:

1. After a unit of study, assign several students to each small group. Each group makes a test about the material. They might include, for example:

    *   true/ false statements

    *   comprehension questions (short-answer, fill-in-the-blank, or multiple-choice)

    *   matching lists (characters with actions, characters with attributes, causes with effects, events with dates, vocabulary with definitions or synonyms)

    *   essay questions

> Online: Put several students in each breakout room.

2. Circulate, offering help.

3. Collect the test items from each group as they finish.

> Online: Students submit their test items to you by email or post them on the discussion board.

4. For the test in the following class session, assemble selected items from the groups' work. Dictate these, type them for distribution, or write them on the board.

> Online: Students return to the main room.

 After the test, you can save yourself time and put students in charge of their own learning by having them correct their own papers. See "Homework or Quiz Review I: Seek and Find" (page 25), "Homework or Quiz Review II: Pairs Do the Correcting" (page 26), and Homework or Quiz Review III: Stand and Deliver (page 26).

4.14 FIND A SENTENCE

"In-reading" tasks can make the difference between students reading mechanically or reading with real interest and comprehension. This activity can be used again and again.

LEVEL: Intermediate – Advanced

AIMS: Reading with a purpose, scanning for information, generating discussion, getting to know classmates

Procedure:

1. Tell students, "While you are reading this, I want you to choose one sentence and write it down to share with the class." You might offer students one or more of these options, depending on the reading:

   • a sentence the student doesn't understand

   • a very interesting sentence

   • a surprising sentence

   • a sentence that contains the main idea

   • a beautiful sentence

   • a sentence that reminds the student of something

   • a sentence that makes great sense to the student

   • a sentence the student agrees or disagrees with

   • a sentence that upsets the student

   Note: The first option above is particularly effective because often when students slow down to identify a sentence they think they don't understand, they suddenly understand it!

2. You have choices here.

   a. Students may write the sentence they chose on the board for class discussion.

   b. In small groups, students share their sentences, telling why they chose that sentence.

   > Online: Put several students in each breakout room.

4.15 GROUP SUMMARIZING

Summarizing activates students' best reading strategies. This activity provides peer support.

LEVEL: Intermediate – Advanced

AIMS: Reading to summarize, speaking about the reading

EQUIPMENT: Document camera/projector or a computer-plus-projector station

Procedure:

1. Divide a reading into sections.

2. Assign each section to a small group of students. (Groups of three work best.)

> Online: Post on your course site a different section of the reading for each breakout room. Put a few students in each breakout room.

3. Each group appoints a secretary and two spokespersons.

4. Students silently read the passages assigned to them.

5. Working together, each group summarizes their passage.

6. The secretaries write their group's main points on the board or on a piece of paper that can be projected using a document camera.

> Online: Students write their main points on a document which can be shared.

7. The spokespersons come to the front of the room together and help each other explain their summary to the class. As a class, discuss what some good titles for this reading might be.

> Online: Students return to the main room and share their documents with the class.

 You may want to follow this with activity 4.13 (Student-Made Tests) or 4.17 (Change the Format).

4.16 SCRAMBLE THE READING

This activity is a fun way to help students notice conjunctions, prepositions, and other links between sentences. It will help them in reading — and in their own writing!

 LEVEL: Intermediate – Advanced

AIM: Using coherence clues to re-order scrambled sentences

MATERIALS: Choose a reading with clear links between sentences. Students will cut the sentences apart and put them back in coherent order.

Procedure:

1. Give every student a copy of the reading. They cut or tear it into individual sentences and mix these up.

> Online: Post the reading on your course site in a format that students can edit. They cut and paste the sentences to scramble them.

Procedure (continued):

2. In pairs, students exchange their scrambled sentences and put them back into correct order.

> Online: Put a pair in each breakout room. They share their documents with each other to unscramble their partner's sentences.

3. Show the original reading so students can confirm whether they have the sentences in the right order.

> Online: Students return to the main room.

4. Discuss with your class the clues that helped them.

4.17 CHANGE THE FORMAT

This activity sparks creativity and leads to deep comprehension. It is effective - and fun - for students to change the prose they have read to a different format.

With "Change the Format," students activate their best reading strategies because they aren't just answering comprehension questions for a teacher who already knows the answers, which is always an artificial interaction. Instead, and much more engaging, students use the information in the reading to produce something original.

LEVEL: Intermediate – Advanced
AIM: Improving reading comprehension

Procedure:

1. Choose a text students have read. It may be fiction or nonfiction. Ask them to change the information from prose to something else. They may work individually, in pairs or groups, or as a class. Students might:

   • Create a timeline of the events.

   • Draw illustrations.

   • Make a chart or graph about the information.

   • Write a poem, song, jazz chant, or rap based on what they read.

   • Create a conversation that could have occurred between two or more of the characters.

   • Make a commercial for something they have read. Stand up and convince the class why everyone should read it.

   • Act out the content.

   • Make a comic book or graphic novel about all or part of the reading.

> Online: If students are working in pairs or groups, assign them to breakout rooms.

Procedure (continued):

Note: Reversing the "direction" of some of the tasks listed on page 54 works just as well! For example, students might:

a.   look at a bus schedule, then write a narrative about someone's adventures traveling

b.   read a menu and write an account of someone's delicious (or disgusting, or unusual) meal

c.   read a chart and write an analysis of the issue/problem.

2.   Students share what they have produced.

> Online: Bring students back to the main room if they are working in breakout rooms.

4.18 READING WITH HALF THE WORDS

Most students become anxious if they find words they don't know in a reading. This activity demonstrates how much they can understand after reading only 50 percent of the words.

LEVEL: Intermediate – Advanced

AIM: Building confidence in reading ability

MATERIALS: A short reading that is a little below the students' level. Here's is what it will look like. You will read the left half aloud to your students. They will not see this, only hear it. At the end of the activity, you might or might not choose to show the class the full reading.

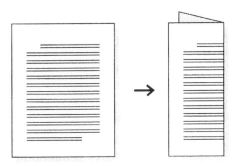

Procedure:

1.   Acknowledge with your students that it can be scary to see new words they don't know in a reading. Tell them, "We are going to do a little experiment to see how many words we really need to understand."

2.   Hold up a copy of the reading. Rip it in half dramatically from top to bottom. Crumple the right-hand side and throw it over your shoulder.

3.   Read the left-hand set of words aloud to the whole class. Your oral reading will sound silly because you are putting in a brief pause at the end of each chopped-off line.

Procedure (continued):

4. Ask students what they understood. If you don't get a lot of immediate volunteers, here are some useful prompts:

   a. Yes/no questions, e.g., "Was this about astronomy?" ("No! It's about farming in Africa.") "Does this story have a sad ending? ("No, he got a lot of money.")

   b. Short-answer questions, e.g., "What is the big problem?" ("There isn't enough water for the farms.") "How many characters are in this story?" ("Three: Amos, his grandfather, and his teacher – oh, and his dog! The dog is important.")

   c. Open-ended questions, e.g.: "What else?" "Tell me one more thing."

5. When the class has collectively recalled/guessed as much as they can, congratulate them! Point out that if they can understand so much after reading only half the words, maybe understanding every word is not very important after all. There is no need to show the whole reading, but if they beg for it, show it to confirm that they already understood enough.

> Online: Display or post the whole reading for the students only if they insist on seeing it.

6. Ask if they are willing to:

   a. try reading without using their dictionaries so often,

   b. read fast sometimes, even if they don't understand everything, and

   c. read easy things in the target language without stopping, just for fun.

Note: Tell them that researchers have discovered that reading a lot will help them improve all of their language skills faster!

4.19 SHARING WHAT WE READ

Extensive reading for pleasure boosts all the other language skills — it's truly remarkable! In this activity, each student chooses their own easy, high-interest materials to read. Later, in class, they tell why they enjoyed what they read. This often catches their classmates' interest, and they want to read it too!

LEVEL: High Beginning – Advanced

AIMS: Doing extensive reading, sharing interesting readings with classmates

Procedure:

Students find easy, interesting readings.

1. Take students to the children's section of a library. (Adults are happy to read children's books and young adult literature if you tell them you're curious about how these compare with children's books in their own culture.) Invite them to pick up as many books as they can for two quick tests: "Do I like the cover and title?" "Can I easily read one random page in the middle?" If a book fails either test, they put it back on the shelf and keep looking. This is great fun!

Note: Students may find other easy readings on their own.

Procedure (continued):

2. Each student chooses three interesting, easy books to read. Here are a few tips:

   - Students often find books about something they already know about. This is great; they'll be reading to confirm meaning, not to decipher it!

   - Many fairy tales are known across cultures, sometimes with interesting differences.

   - Side-by-side translations are wonderful if you can find them.

   > Online: Show students how to access an online library for Steps 1 and 2.

In class: students explore the collection.

3. If possible, set up big tables in the middle of an open space. (You could spread a clean sheet on the floor to make a big surface.)

4. Students lay out all the things they've been reading. When every student puts out three to six books or other easy readings, it's quite a display!

5. Students circle around the collection for 10 minutes or so, briefly handling as many books as they can. They are getting ready to choose one they might want to read themselves.

   > Online: For Steps 3, 4, and 5, put three to five students in each breakout room to share the titles they've read.

Show and Tell time! Students talk about what they read.

6. With all readings returned to the center space, students step back and decide what their favorite reading is. At your signal, everyone picks up something from the collection.

7. Students find the "owner" (they may have to hold their chosen reading up high and call out: "Whose is this!")

8. Students mingle. Speaking with one classmate at a time, the 'owner' tells why they liked that reading. Pairs talk briefly and then return it to the collection. This stage may go on for quite a while, with students choosing reading after reading and discussing it briefly with the owner.

9. (Optional) Students may ask to borrow one another's readings. The authors used this for many years, and no one lost a book.

   > Online: For steps 6-9, students remain in their breakout rooms. After everyone has discussed the books they've read, the students identify which of the other students' books they are interested in.

4.20 MARK THE MARGINS

This "in-reading" activity activates students' best reading strategies by requiring them to respond with margin notes as they read. Students understand more because they're responding to content as they go along.

It also helps them stay on task because their margin marks are visible to the teacher. Most important, using this routine regularly helps students gain confidence and independence as readers.

LEVEL: High Beginning – Advanced

AIM: Activating students' strategies while they are reading

Procedure:

1. Give students a reading.

2. Depending on your reading, choose one of the boxes below. Students write those symbols in the margins as they read. If it's not appropriate for students to write directly on what they're reading, they can lay or tape a strip of blank paper beside the text and mark on that.

> Online: Students can insert symbols in the reading file by using the "insert comments" feature in Adobe Acrobat or Microsoft Word, for example.

A	I already do this
M	I want to do this more
?	Other response (e.g. I don't understand, or not applicable)

✓	I understand
?	I don't understand

ME	This reminds me of something that happened to me.

For the margins beside the word problemns in math, students can list the operations they'll use to solve the problem, then compare these notes with a classmate before going ahead with the calculations

+	add
-	substract
x	multiply
÷	divide

A	I agree
D	I disagree
N	I have no opinion yet

C	cause
E	effect

F	fact
O	writer's opinion

I	Interesting to me

N	New to me.
A	I already knew this
T.	I can teach this to somebody

3. Students who finish early mingle and discuss their margin marks with classmates while slower readers get the time they need to finish. Students are interested to see that people have different responses to the same reading.

> Online: Put early finishers in a breakout room. Students can send you a message in the chat when they are finished.

4.21 REPORTER/WRITER

Sometimes a bit of competition is fun! In this holistic dictation activity, one student in each pair, the "reporter," runs back and forth. They read something you've posted on the wall, then dash back to their seated partner, the "writer," and dictate what's on the wall.

LEVEL: Beginning – Advanced

AIMS: Reading and writing about a paragraph or picture, building vocabulary, checking grammar, speaking clearly, listening for specific information

MATERIALS: A short, simple paragraph or picture(s). For a large class, you'll need to have one copy for approximately every four students so everyone can see it well.

Procedure:

1. Post copies of a detailed picture or a paragraph on the wall outside the class. It must be at least ten steps away from where students are sitting.

    > Online: Later, in Step 3, you will share your screen to show the picture or paragraph.

2. Put students in pairs. One student will be the reporter and one the writer.

    > Online: Put a pair in each breakout room.

3. The reporters all stand up and walk swiftly to what's on the wall. It's at least ten steps away, so the reporters have to process it deeply. If the reading is closer than ten steps away, they don't need to process the meaning: it becomes a short-term memory exercise. The reporters go back and forth to the wall until they have dictated everything to their partner.

    > Online: Share your screen to show the picture or paragraph. The reporters will return to the main room to see what you posted. Tell them to carry as much information in their minds as possible before returning to their writing partner.

4. They hurry to their partners and report what they read or saw. Tell them to keep their hands clasped behind their backs, so they're not tempted to take over the writer's job.

    > Online: The reporters go back to their breakout rooms.

5. The writer tries to write exactly what the reporter tells them. Errors usually creep in.

    > Online: The writers share their screens and type what the reporters tell them.

6. The reporter dashes back and forth, reading and reporting, until the writing partner has it all on paper.

Procedure (continued):

7. Partners sit together to look at what the writer wrote. They negotiate and discuss words, word order, spelling, and grammar.

> Online: Both partners stay in their breakout room.

8. Give each pair of students a copy of the posted paragraph or picture to check. They can immediately self-correct their own mistakes. You have created a powerful learning moment!

> Online: Post the picture or paragraph so that the whole class can see it. Both the reporter and writer view it to check their work.

Acknowledgment: This is a variation of an activity we learned from Mario Rinvolucri during a conference.

Chapter Five

Writing

Writing lets us communicate across space and time. We write to fill out a job application. We write to leave a note for a friend. Even the act of writing our own name is a step into empowerment in a new language. Eventually, we write to organize, even to discover, our own ideas. We write to express ourselves.

Writing is the most challenging of the language skills for students, and it can be the most time-consuming work a teacher does. This chapter aims to help!

5.1 QUICK-WRITE

This writing fluency activity stimulates imagination. It helps students get over their nervousness about writing and leap beyond the barrier of writer's block.

LEVEL: Intermediate – Advanced
AIMS: Generating ideas, pushing through writer's block

Procedure:

1. Tell students, "I'm going to give you a topic to write about. You will have five minutes. Fill up a paper with as many sentences as possible. I won't be collecting your papers. It's OK if you make a lot of mistakes. If you can't think of a word you need, leave a blank space or put in a word from another language. If you don't have any ideas, keep your pen moving like this (draw a spiral from left to right on the board) until your next idea comes to you. The only rule is: Don't stop writing! Keep your pen moving!"

> Online: Use an application or program such as Microsoft Teams or Google Docs that will allow you to see students' writing instantly/synchronously.

2. Dictate an unfinished sentence. This might be related to a reading or discussion, to the students' lives, or to a composition they will be writing soon. For fun, have students propose their own high-interest topics sometimes. Here is a menu of some topics that get students excited:

    *   When I remember my school days…
    *   When I think of vacations, I…
    *   I'll never forget the time I lost…
    *   Sometimes you just have to tell a lie because…
    *   I just hate it when people…
    *   The person I admire most is…
    *   I get very upset when…
    *   I really needed help when…
    *   The best present I ever gave someone was…
    *   The best present I ever got was…
    *   I feel frightened when…
    *   I felt like a real success when…
    *   A dream that I have for my country is…
    *   The most serious problem in the world today is…
    *   The best way to cure a cold is…

3. While students are writing, it's best to keep your distance. Don't circulate among them; your presence may reawaken their nervousness about making mistakes. If anyone stops writing for more than ten seconds, catch that student's eye and point to the spiral on the board. They should keep their pen moving.

> Online: Discreetly check each students' documents to make sure students are writing without stopping.

Procedure (continued):

4. When the five minutes are up, invite students to hold up their papers to display how much they have written. Congratulate them!

> Online: Invite a few students to share their screens.

5. Ask students what is helpful about this activity. Accept all their answers and be sure to bring up the point that we don't need to have ideas all complete in our minds before we write. Writing fast is one way to discover ideas.

5.2 ONE-MINUTE FEEDBACK

Why wait for the end of the course to find out from our students what they are learning? In this activity, students do a brief review at the end of class and write you a note about one thing they learned.

When they do this, students pay more attention to what they understand and don't understand during class. They take more responsibility for their learning and ask more questions because they know they will be writing you this note. Another benefit: when students review at the end of class, they remember more.

A quick review of their cards after class lets you know what you need to clarify or reteach next time. Best of all, you get to see what your students DID learn. This feels like a pat on the back, something we get too little of!

LEVEL: Beginning – Advanced
AIMS: Getting feedback from students about what they are learning
MATERIALS: 3 or 4 blank index cards for each student to start with. They will buy more for themselves.

Procedure:

1. When students come into class, hand each a card. Tell them that at the end of class you will ask them to write on the card what they learned today and give the card to you.

> Online: Students can submit their notes by email.

2. Allow a minute or so at the end of class for each student to glance back at what they've done in class and write their feedback note to you.

3. Collect their notes. Because the time is so short, students are concise, and you need only a few minutes after class to read their notes and incorporate what they have said into your planning.

5.3 BUDDY JOURNALS

Extensive writing, even when it's not corrected, helps students write better. In this activity, students free-write on interesting topics while the teacher has time to give individual attention to those who need it.

LEVEL: Intermediate – Advanced

AIMS: Practicing free writing, getting to know one another, reading classmates' journal entries

MATERIALS: A list of topics you can suggest if a student says they have nothing to write about

Procedure:

1. Early in your course, ask students to purchase notebooks for journals and to write their names in them. Collect these from time to time and write a brief response. This helps students be accountable without adding much work for you.

   > Online: Create an online space where students can save their documents, and you can access them. You can set this up using products such as Google Drive or Microsoft OneDrive, or your course's learning management system.

2. At the beginning of the course, give students some suggested topics for them to list in the front of the journals. They use this if they occasionally can't think of something to write about.

   > Online: Post this list where students can access it throughout the course.

   Possible topics (students can suggest others):
   - Foods I Love
   - A Favorite Vacation
   - What I Want in a Good Friend
   - Something I Am Proud Of
   - A Book or Film I Loved
   - What's Wrong With the World Today?
   - The Way I Feel About Money
   - My Ideal House
   - A Difficult Decision I Made
   - My Favorite Relative

3. At the beginning of each week, tell students they will be writing about their lives in their journals. Announce which day they will do this in class.

4. On the assigned day, give an extended time for journal writing.

5. Put students in pairs. They exchange journals with their partners and write positive responses to what their partner has written.

   > Online: Partners share their journal entries with each other. Each student looks at their partner's journal entry and writes responses directly on that digital document.

5.4 PEER REVISION I: WHAT I THINK YOU SAID

This remarkable peer-review routine focuses on meaning rather than editorial details. It quickly helps students clarify what they wrote. A side benefit is that pronunciation improves as authors/readers struggle to make themselves understood.

LEVEL: High Beginning – Advanced

AIMS: Revising classmates' compositions, listening to retell, paraphrasing information, improving pronunciation

Procedure:

Prior to this Activity

1. Students produce a piece of writing for homework or in class.

Demonstration Stage

2. Bring up two students to model what everyone is about to do in pairs. Ask Student A to start reading their composition to Student B. Guide A to read enough at a time so that B can't use short-term memory to parrot back what they heard. B must understand a chunk of meaning and then re-tell it in their own words.

3. Each time A reads a bit more and B re-tells what they understood A to say, encourage A to respond with phrases such as

    "Yes, that's right!"

    "Yes, and I also said.... "

    "Partly correct. Here's what I really meant: .... "

    "No, that's not what I tried to say. Let me explain."

Write these on the board for the whole class to practice orally.

> Online: Post the model responses in the chat or elsewhere for students to view during the activity.

Now the pairs get to work!

4. A reads their composition and B paraphrases as they go along.

> Online: Put a pair in each breakout room.

5. The partners switch. Now B reads their composition, getting feedback from A.

6. Often, what the author/reader says during this activity is clearer than what they wrote! Together, the pair discusses what changes in the writing will make the meaning clearer. The author/reader, of course, is the final judge of what to change.

7. As a class, volunteers may share an example of how their writing got better.

> Online: Students return to the main room before sharing.

5.5 PEER REVISION II: IMPROVING WRITTEN WORK IN PAIRS

When students help one another by improving their written work together, it is immediately clear that the writer is being helped by a classmate. The hidden benefit — which soon becomes clear to students — is that when they help a classmate, their own written work begins to have fewer errors. The detachment of working on someone else's paper allows them to notice errors more easily, and they begin spotting more errors in their own writing.

This activity will save you a great deal of time because students correct their work before handing it in to you.

 Before doing this activity, students may use "Editing and Revision: I Can Do It Myself" (Activity 5.10) to review their personal lists of common errors.

 LEVEL: Beginning – Advanced
AIMS: Revising compositions

Procedure:

1. Write on the board a list of things to look for in peer editing. Students copy this as you write. Here are some ideas you might include. You will, of course, know what you want your own students to focus on.

   Revision:

   1. Does my composition answer the assigned question?
   2. Is it easy for my reader to understand?
   3. Did I organize my ideas clearly?
   4. Did I provide enough supporting details?
   5. Is each paragraph clearly about one central idea?
   6. Do I have a clear introduction?
   7. Do I have a logical conclusion?

   Editing:

   8. Did I write a title?
   9. Did I capitalize important words in the title?
   10. Did I indent every paragraph?
   11. Does every sentence have a capital letter and a period or other punctuation?
   12. Did I use correct verb forms in every sentence?
   13. (Add other things you want your students to focus on.)

   Note: Most people can't focus effectively on more than one idea at a time. Tell students to reread the compositions they edit several times, each time focusing on just one item from the list.

2. In pairs, students review the peer editing responses of one composition first, then the other, before handing them in to you.

Procedure (continued):

Note: It is important to use words like *help* and *improve* in your instructions, rather than *look for errors* or *correct*. For example, say: "Let's make sure this is our best work. I'll give you some time to help each other improve your work before you hand it in."

> Online: Put a pair in each breakout room.

3. As the pairs work, circulate and continue to use this positive language. Some students are reluctant to point out classmates' errors for fear of being rude, and nobody likes to feel criticized. They are much more willing to give and receive help if they have encouragement that opens them up to it.

> Online: Circulate to each breakout room to encourage the use of positive language.

4. As a class, students may discuss what they learned while working with their classmate.

> Online: Students return to the main room before sharing.

5.6 THREE UNRELATED THINGS

This activity unleashes creativity as each student creates their own story based on three random prompts. Comparing the stories afterward is great fun!

LEVEL: Intermediate – Advanced
AIMS: Writing a creative story, reading classmates' stories aloud

Procedure:

1. As a class, ask students to name three things that might be in a story but have no relationship to each other. For example, students might suggest a snake, a piece of dirty paper, and falling down. Write these on the board.
2. Tell students they will write a creative story that includes all three things.
3. Silently, students write their stories.
4. Pairs read these to each other and work together on both papers to correct errors.

> Online: Put a pair in each breakout room.

5. Display these on the wall for everyone to walk around and read.

> Online: Students post their stories on the discussion board.

6. Each student chooses one story (not their own) to read aloud.
7. After the class has heard a few of these, they say which one they like the best.

> Online: Students return to the main room before sharing.

Procedure (continued):

Variation (speaking option): Instead of writing, you may want students to just tell their stories. After Step 1, pairs tell each other their stories. Then put two pairs together; now you have groups of four. Everyone retells their own story (this second telling goes better) and listens to three other stories. Groups choose one story for presentation to the whole class.

> Online: Put a pair in each breakout room. After a short time, shuffle the breakout rooms so that each room has four students. Then students return to the main room to share one story from each group.

An Introduction to Dictocomps

A Dictocomp is a combination of dictation and composition. We have found it indispensable! Dictocomps provide excellent practice in close listening, writing, and reading.

Dictocomps offer two great advantages:
- personalized learning because every student makes different mistakes
- immediate feedback: you work less, and students learn more!

The basic Dictocomp is quite simple:
1. Read a passage aloud slowly. Students do not look at the reading. Repeat a few times, increasing to normal speed. Students listen closely and write a small number of key words as notes. These words may be chosen by the teacher or by each individual student. They will serve as prompts when students recreate the passage in writing. Ask the class to tell you when they've heard enough to understand the reading well.
2. Students write the whole passage as well as they can.
3. Provide feedback. This depends on your aims; you'll find good options in the activities that follow.

Two ways to use Dictocomps:
A. If the purpose of the activity is to practice specific vocabulary or language, choose a reading with words students have been studying, or focus on specifics such as spelling, grammar, punctuation, or sentence structure.
B. On the other hand, if the purpose is to develop general composition skills, students will be writing to paraphrase the message in their own words. This broader outcome gives you more flexibility when choosing a passage.

How to end a Dictocomp:
A. If your focus was on specific vocabulary/language features (point A above), finish this activity by having students look at the original reading to self-correct their mistakes.
B. If your objective was to develop broader writing skills (point B above), students do NOT refer to the original reading to culminate this activity. We don't want them to self-correct something that may be just a different way to express an idea. Instead, they may compare their work in pairs, groups, or a class discussion. Let the small details go. The focus today is on good paraphrasing and revision.

5.7 DICTOCOMP: KEY WORDS ON THE BOARD

In this activity, you provide key words as scaffolding to help students reconstruct a reading. Students help one another and finally look at the reading to correct anything they missed. Everyone makes their own mistakes and gets immediate feedback, so there's no need for you to collect and mark a single paper!

LEVEL: High Beginning – Advanced

AIMS: Writing what you hear, paraphrasing information, listening for specific information

Procedure:

Pre-teach Vocabulary

1. Choose any short reading passage (a single sentence or a paragraph).

2. Write several key vocabulary items on the board. Clarify the meanings of these words (Students can help!)

The Dictocomp

3. Read the passage aloud slowly. It is not visible to students.

4. Read the passage again at a normal pace.

5. Using the words on the board as prompts, students write out the full passage, trying to get it as close as possible to the original.

Assessment

6. In pairs, students compare their papers, adding or correcting as needed.

> Online: Put a pair in each breakout room.

7. Students refer to the reading and make final corrections.

> Online: Make the passage available.

Whole Class Wrap Up

8. As a class, volunteers may talk about something they learned from the exercise.

> Online: Students return to the main room before sharing.

5.8 ACTING-OUT DICTOCOMP

This activity wakes up a class and is particularly useful with writing passages that involve a procedure. In this Dictocomp, the aim is accuracy (in spelling, punctuation, etc.) Students correct their own writing by looking at the passage.

LEVEL: Beginning – Intermediate

AIMS: Listening for details, reconstructing a passage from key words, writing with correct spelling and punctuation

Procedure:

1. Choose a reading passage that involves a series of actions. Some examples are getting up in the morning, starting a car, getting on an airplane, preparing a meal, finding an apartment

2. Read the passage aloud slowly. It is not visible to students.

3. After each action, elicit key words from the class. Put these on the board.

4. Reread the passage at normal speed two or three times.

5. Mime the passage as students look at the key words and write down each of your actions.

6. Individually, students write out the passage as completely as they can.

7. Students look at the passage to correct their writing.

> Online: Display the passage.

5.9 DICTOCOMP: STUDENTS REMEMBER THE KEY WORDS

This variation of Dictocomp emphasizes meaning, not accuracy with details like spelling or punctuation. Praise students when they create good paraphrases and use reasonable synonyms.

LEVEL: Intermediate – Advanced
AIMS: Listening for details, paraphrasing

Procedure:

1. Choose any new paragraph that is not too long or too hard.

2. Read the paragraph three times. Increase speed with each reading, but do not exceed normal speed. The paragraph is not visible to students.

3. Reread the paragraph a fourth time. This time leave out about five to ten key words. Say "blank" or make a sound like "hmmmm" in place of each missing word.

4. As you go along, students list the words they think you left out.

5. Each student writes the paragraph as well as they can, using their list of words as prompts.

6. Because your aim is for students to recreate meaning in their own words, they do not look at the paragraph. Instead, they do the following two steps:

   a. Students work in small groups to rewrite the passage together, producing a single paper.

   > Online: Put a few students in each breakout room.

   b. One member from each group reads the group's paragraph to the whole class. Praise all good paraphrasing!

   > Online: Students return to the main room before sharing.

5.10 EDITING AND REVISION: I CAN DO IT MYSELF

With this activity, students learn to recognize and correct their "old" errors before they hand in a piece of writing. This powerful routine transforms the work of teaching composition in three ways:

- When students catch their own errors, you have far fewer mistakes to mark in their papers. This saves you many hours of work!
- You can pay attention to the new errors students make as they explore the "interlanguage" zone between their native language and the target language. This is where learning happens.
- Finally, as students take responsibility for consistently applying what they have learned, they see how much their writing improves. It's a great confidence booster!

LEVEL: High Beginning – Advanced

AIMS: Improving students' ability to edit their own work

MATERIALS: A two-pocket folder for each student. This will hold formal compositions only — no other work. You can use it throughout your course.

> Online: Create an online space where students can save their documents, and you can access them. You can use products such as Google Drive or Microsoft OneDrive, or your course's learning management system to create these portfolio folders.

Procedure:

Establishing the Routine

1. Ask students what they each can already do correctly in their compositions. Depending on the level, you might suggest such things as centering a title at the top of the page, indenting paragraphs, making sure subjects and verbs agree, using a spelling checker or making sure each paragraph has a topic sentence. Choose a few of these ideas to write on the board to help students start brainstorming.

2. At the top of a piece of paper, students write their name and this sentence: "Things I already know and can always do correctly." At the bottom of that paper, they write, "If I check all these things, I am ready to give my writing to my teacher." They staple this paper inside the folder. See graphic below.

> Online: Students will type these two sentences in an online document and save it in their digital portfolio folder.

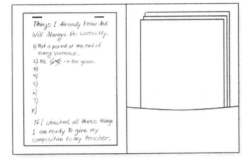

Procedure (continued):

3. Explain that this routine will help them let go of old mistakes while making new ones. Assure them that you will help them, and their writing will improve fast!

Using the Folders: This is the routine you will use throughout your course.

4. Students write the number "1" on their paper (under the header "Things I Already Know...") and write something they know they can always do correctly. They will continue listing more things throughout your course. Each student lists only what they're confident they will never do incorrectly in a paper they hand in to you.

5. Their papers become a portfolio as they add successive drafts of assigned compositions throughout your course. When a student masters something, invite them to add it to the list in their folder. Note: It is important that each student, not you, chooses what goes on their list.

6. Before students hand in each composition, give them class time to use their lists in editing their work. Peers can help. Encourage them to look for only one thing at a time. This will take some modeling and persistence until students notice for themselves how many errors they miss when they try to keep several things in mind at the same time.

> Online: If students want peer help, put them in a breakout room together to share their writing.

Keeping the Standards High

7. When students finally hand in a piece of writing, each one has taken responsibility for the errors on their personal lists. When you find an error that a student has claimed mastery of but appears anyway, you have options.

    a. You may (or may not) automatically lower the grade. This sounds harsh but quickly sets a new standard to help students be more careful about applying what they know.

    b. If a student is usually conscientious but somehow missed one error, you may decide to write in the margin the number of that error from the student's list, perhaps adding a question mark or a friendly "oops!" Conscientious students will pay particular attention to that error next time.

> Online: Insert the error number, question mark or a friendly "oops!" in their document.

You will know best how to handle this with your own students but remember that keeping the standards high will pay off in a huge reduction of the time you spend grading papers. At the same time, students will be proud of their work and of themselves.

Note: With this activity, students are creating portfolios with proof that they are continually leaving behind old errors and writing better. This is very satisfying! Even advanced students, who can become jaded when their language development reaches a "plateau," often respond to this routine with renewed motivation to write better.

5.11 REMEMBER THE PICTURE

In this activity, students generate sentences from a picture and edit them to make them structurally correct.

LEVEL: Intermediate – Advanced

AIMS: Composing structurally correct sentences, writing about a picture, proofreading for correct sentence structure

MATERIALS: Any interesting picture

Procedure:

1. Ask the class, "What is a sentence?" Elicit their ideas and write a useful working definition on the board, for example, "A sentence is a group of words that makes sense together, expresses a complete thought, and includes a subject and a verb."

2. Show an interesting picture with many details. Say, "Try to remember everything in this picture." After everyone gets a good look, put the picture away. Tell students they will write as many complete and correct sentences about the picture as they can.

> Online: Share your screen to show the picture, and then stop screen sharing.

3. Divide your class into small groups. Each group gives itself a name.

> Online: Put small groups in each breakout room.

4. In their groups, students generate as many sentences as they can about the picture. A recorder writes sentences as they work.

5. Send some recorders to the board. They write the sentences their group has produced.

> Online: Students return to the main room. Some recorders share their screen.

6. While the recorders are writing, the class looks for incorrect or incomplete sentences.

7. Help students identify sentences that are not acceptable. Correct these. Only sentences that are grammatically and factually correct stay up on the board.

> Online: As students share their screen, they correct sentences that are not acceptable.

Supercharge Your Teaching!

Want to maximize the power of group work? Give students a clear TASK, GOAL, and TIME. For more tips, see "Effective Group Work" in our free guide *Supercharge Your Teaching* downloadable from ProLinguaLearning.com.

5.12 WRITTEN ARGUMENT

This activity generates a lot of laughter as students write. What makes this activity particularly interesting is that students are forced to see both sides of an issue.

LEVEL: Intermediate – Advanced

AIMS: Writing a dialogue, performing a role-play dialogue, learning to see an argument from multiple points of view

Procedure:

1. Students sit in a circle. Each student has paper and something to write with.

   > Online: Students remain in the main room, without needing to sit in a circle.

2. Tell them the following story, perhaps adjusting language level for some classes: "You are the roommate of someone who never cleans the room that the two of you live in. Your roommate is a brilliant student who keeps promising you that they will do their share in cleaning, but somehow, they always forget. It is true that they frequently help you with your studies, and this is why, most of the time, you have forgiven them for not cleaning.

   However, this time things have gone too far. You had to go away for the weekend, and your roommate promised you that they would clean the room. Now it is Monday morning. You have just returned, and you have to rush to class. When you walk into the room, you see a horrendous mess: papers all over, leftover food on the desk, beds unmade, dust everywhere. The place stinks! As you stand there, the door opens, and your roommate walks in." Tell students, "Please write the first thing you would say as the clean roommate."

3. Students are eager to write! After they've written a sentence or two, say, "Please finish the sentence you are writing. Do not begin a new sentence."

4. Everyone passes their papers to the right and receives a paper from their classmate to their left. They read what their classmate just wrote as the clean roommate.

   > Online: Put three to four students in each breakout room. Each student shares their sentences with another student using the chat or email. Students will give their sentences to one student and receive them from another (this is why the groups need at least three students).

5. On this new paper, they write their answer in the role of the messy roommate.

6. When you tell them it is time, students pass their papers back to the original writer. They now write as the clean roommate again.

7. Students continue passing their papers back and forth as long as they are having fun. They are creating two dialogues.

Procedure (continued):

8. Pairs of students volunteer to act out a dialogue, with praise and suggestions from the class after each performance.

> Online: Students return to the main room to share their dialogues.

Note: You can use this role-play technique for any kind of argument-related topic or situation. For example:

a. generating ideas for a student's real problem (Perhaps Ali has to go downtown to contest a speeding ticket tomorrow, or Maria needs her deposit back from her reluctant landlord.)

b. creating a dialogue between two angry characters from a story, movie, or TV program

c. preparing for a debate by arguing two sides of a controversial topic

Acknowledgment: This is a variation of an activity we learned from Mario Rinvolucri during an IATEFL (International Association for the Teaching of English as a Foreign Language) conference.

5.13 IMAGINARY GIFT EXCHANGE

As much as we enjoy receiving presents, it can be an even greater pleasure to give a well-chosen gift. This activity helps to build a friendly classroom climate and is as much fun for students as giving and receiving real presents. Use this after students have gotten to know one another or at the end of a course.

LEVEL: High Beginning – Advanced

AIMS: Writing friendly notes, expressing gratitude for a gift, building classroom community

MATERIALS: A container for slips of paper

Procedure:

1. To make sure everyone gets presents, students put their names on slips of paper and drop them all into the container.

2. Tell students, "Today we are giving one another imaginary presents, so you can give whatever you want! For example, you can give someone extra time." As a class, create a list on the board of some things they might want to give and receive.

3. On the board write the following formulas:

> Dear_____,
>
> I would like to give you _____ for a present because_____.
>
> Yours,
>
> ____

Procedure (continued):

> Dear _____
>
> Thanks so much for_____. I like it because _____.
>
> Sincerely,
>
> _____

4. Students pick a name from the container and get busy sending that person a "present." That is, everyone writes a "present" note.

> Online: Tell students individually/discretely in the chat to whom each student should give a present.

5. When a student finishes their "present" note, they fold it and deliver it to their classmate. If students still have time, they can write another "present" note to a student of their choice.

> Online: Students send their notes directly to their classmate in the chat box.

6. Each time a student receives a "present" note, they immediately write and deliver a thank-you note.

> Online: Students send their thank-you notes directly to their classmate in the chat box.

7. Students talk to the whole class about their "presents," ones they gave and/or ones they received.

5.14 WHO IS THIS?

Students love this activity because they get to see some positive things their classmates notice about them. It's good writing practice because it encourages students to notice details and make their written language clear and specific.

LEVEL: Intermediate – Advanced
AIMS: Writing descriptions, listening for specific details, recycling vocabulary, building classroom community
MATERIALS: A small container

Procedure:

1. To make sure everyone gets described, students put their names on slips of paper and drop them all into the container. Students choose a name at random.

> Online: Tell students individually/discretely in the chat who each student should describe.

Procedure (continued):

2. Students write a positive description of the classmate they have chosen. They might include physical details or personality traits. Encourage them to be as detailed as possible but not to mention the name.

3. In pairs, students read their descriptions aloud to each other. Encourage listeners to pay attention to the entire description. Listeners guess who the description is about and tell which detail in the description was most revealing.

> Online: Students take turns reading their descriptions out loud, and the class guesses who is being described.

4. Students give their classmate the description they wrote. Give everyone plenty of time to smile.

> Online: Students take turns reading their descriptions out loud, and the class guesses who is being described.

5. Continue with additional rounds of this activity as long as students are enjoying it.

5.15 FACES

This activity stimulates imagination, leads to interesting conversations, and shows students how quickly we make up our minds about people.

LEVEL: Intermediate – Advanced
AIMS: Writing about a picture, expanding vocabulary
MATERIALS: An interesting picture of a person with the face clearly visible

Procedure:

1. Show the class a picture of a person.

2. Dictate these sentences:

   - "My name is _____"
   - "I live in _____ with_____."
   - "Recently, I have been very happy because _____"
   - "I used to_____, but now I _____."
   - "I have changed my mind about _____ "
   - "Today is my birthday. All I really want is _____."
   - You can choose other sentences if you wish.

3. Students complete the sentences by writing what they imagine to be true about the person in the picture.

4. Students sit in small groups and take turns reading their sentences to one another.

> Online: Put a few students in each breakout room.

5. Each group chooses their favorite sentences and reads them to the whole class.

> Online: Students return to the main room before sharing.

6. As a class, students talk about how and why they made up their minds about the people in the picture. This usually leads to interesting discussions of stereotypes and first impressions.

5.16 WRITING THE END OF A STORY

This activity sparks creativity as students listen to the beginning of a story and then write original conclusions.

LEVEL: Intermediate – Advanced
AIMS: Listening to a story, writing a story conclusion

Procedure:

1. Begin telling a story. You may choose one you remember, invent one, or read one from a book.
2. Stop at a climactic point. Give students time to think of a conclusion.
3. Students write their conclusions.
4. Pairs read these to each other and work together on both papers to help each other.

> Online: Put a pair in each breakout room. Students share their screen to show what they wrote.

5. Display these on the wall for everyone to walk around and read.

> Online: Students post their conclusions on the discussion board.

6. Each student chooses one conclusion (not their own). Volunteers read some of these aloud for everyone to enjoy.

 This activity works well after "Finish the Story" (Chapter 3, page 28)

5.17 FREE-ASSOCIATION POEMS

This activity sparks imagination, generates new vocabulary, and can give students a new way of seeing one another.

LEVEL: Intermediate – Advanced
AIMS: Expanding vocabulary, encouraging creativity
SETUP: Prepare the list of prompts in Step 4 to show the students.

Procedure:

1. Ask students to look around the room they are in and notice everything they see, from large features such as the ceiling to small things like a piece of chalk or the dust on a chair. (This can become a great opportunity for students to learn some new words from you and from classmates.)

2. Students tell you some of the things they have noticed. Note these on the board; new vocabulary may emerge.

3. Demonstrate: Choose one object from the list. Call on one student at a time to tell the class something this object might say if it could speak. If you have chosen curtains, for example, students might say sentences like these:

   "I am the curtains. I am dusty. I am old. I let the light and heat inside every morning. I keep the room cool in the afternoon. I am very important. People open me, close me, open me, close me every day. But nobody notices me. Nobody notices that I am dirty. Nobody asks me what I want. Someday I will refuse to slide until they say, 'Thank you.'"

4. Getting Ready to Write: Show students a list of prompts. Each student chooses one thing in the room. Ask them to imagine they are this object. To generate ideas, instruct students to whisper a list of statements using these prompts.

   - I am the_____.
   - I am ... (adjective)
   - I am ... (another adjective)
   - I have ...
   - I want ...
   - I never ...
   - I always ...
   - I like ...
   - I hate ...
   - I love ...
   - People _____ me ...
   - Nobody ...
   - I wish ...
   - Someday, ...

They may skip some prompts, use others more than once, or invent new ones.

5. After a couple of minutes, clap your hands to signal that it's time for them to write what they have been whispering to themselves.

6. When most students are finished writing, volunteers read their sentences to the class.

Note: Don't tell the students in advance, but these are often revealing, personal poems. Students tend to project their own feelings onto the chosen object. For this reason, respect students' privacy by letting each student choose whether to read aloud.

> This activity works equally well in an online class with no adaptations.

Chapter Six
Vocabulary

WORDS WORDS WORDS...

"Teacher, I need more words!" It's true. Students know it, and so do we if we've ever studied a new language.

Language learners are constantly meeting new words. They need time to practice with them in class. They also need strategies they can use on their own.

Three Essential Principles for Teaching Vocabulary

1. Teach at all three stages of vocabulary learning. Students at EVERY level — beginner through advanced — go through the same process with a new word: first it's a stranger, then they befriend it, then they get to know it well.

* Stage 1 - Meet the Words: initial exposure to new words

* Stage 2 - Work with Words: manipulating and recycling them

* Stage 3 - Make the Words My Own: deeper understanding and long-term retention

Note: Most teachers unconsciously specialize in one of these stages. Once we're aware of this, we can expand our repertoire and make sure we're providing instruction in all three. This chapter helps you do just that!

2. Decide how many words to teach in a lesson.

* Focus on no more than 5 to 8 words per lesson.

* Throughout your course, individualize as much as possible by giving each student a say in what words – and how many words - they intend to learn.

3. Provide frequent review.

* Spaced learning, with increasing time between reviews, is much more powerful than intensively studying a word. For example, coach students to use their vocabulary cards (page 82) to review their new words after 5 minutes / 25 minutes / 10 hours (or end of day) / one day / one week / one month.

STAGE 1: MEET THE WORDS

6.1 VOCABULARY CARDS

Flashcards are a powerful, personalized strategy for all three stages of vocabulary learning. With a sketch or translation on the back, a card introduces a new word. With more information on the back, it works for Stages 2 and 3.

Some students have a habit of listing words and definitions side by side in two columns. Vocabulary cards are far more effective!

- It's easy for students to add new words and throw away cards once they have mastered a word.

- They're great for review because students see the word but can't see their notes until they turn the card over.

- Students can post cards on their refrigerator, their bathroom mirror, etc. to see them often.

There are online applications similar to physical vocabulary cards, yet there are good reasons why many teachers still prefer physical cards. Because the cards are handwritten, they feel more personal. Because handwriting takes time, new words are better anchored in memory. Finally, because students manipulate the cards with their own hands, multiple intelligences are engaged.

LEVEL: Beginning – Advanced

AIM: Ongoing individual review of new words

MATERIALS: 3 or 4 blank index cards for each student to start with. They will buy more for themselves.

Procedure:

In the center of a 3 X 5 card, students write a new vocabulary word as large as possible, filling up the whole space. On the back, they put things that will help them remember the word. Keep it simple to start with: beginning students may write only a translation or a sketch. At all levels, as students review their cards and come to know the words better, they will add more information such as similar words or opposites, notes about pronunciation or part of speech, etc. Beyond the beginning level, the most important thing that must be on the back of every card is a sentence in the target language using the new word correctly.

Tips for Creating Good Sentences for Vocabulary Cards

Beginners copy sentences from you or a good learner's dictionary. Intermediate and advanced students write their own sentences. These are memorable because they're personal.

Checking all of these is time-consuming and not essential. Instead, use this sampling technique:

1. Each student writes their original sentence with a new word on the back of their card.

Procedure (continued):

2. To help everyone while preserving anonymity, circulate to collect one or more instructive examples. Write these on the board.

> Online: Students send you their sentences privately in the chat. Choose a few instructive examples. Write these on the board.

3. With the whole class, go over the sentences on the board, clarifying where needed.

4. Now that they understand the word better, students often revise the sentences they wrote on their own cards.

This process is student-centered and very effective. It doesn't take much time.

Now that they have good vocabulary cards, students use them as flashcards, quizzing themselves independently (in class and at home). They look at the front of each card, try to remember it and use it in a sentence, and flip to the back if they need help or confirmation.

Great Ways to Use Vocabulary Cards

Students can use vocabulary cards again and again! Here are three ways:

1. In class, pairs quiz each other by playing a card game. They face each other and fan out their flash cards. They see the side with a word, and their partner sees the back side. They take turns lifting out one card from their partner's set. Their partner uses that word in a sentence. If they get it wrong, that card goes back in with the other fanned-out cards. If they get it right, that card is set aside: success! It will be returned for later review after the game.

> Online: Put a pair in each breakout room. Students shuffle their cards and place them face down so only the fronts are showing. One at a time, they close their eyes and choose a random card, holding it up so they can see only the word on the front. Their partner can now see the information on the back. (Don't worry if it's a bit blurry; the activity will still work.)

2. Students take out all their cards and arrange them into categories, then explain to a classmate why they sorted them in this way. (Typical categories might be colors, clothing, parts of speech, easy words/words I need to study more, etc.). Categorizing makes new associations in the brain. No matter what categories a student may choose, the act of sorting makes words more memorable!

> Online: Students arrange their vocabulary words into categories and type them in a document. (This can be done as homework.) In class, put a pair in each breakout room to share their categories with their partners.

3. Want a clever way to save time creating and grading quizzes? Just choose a few random vocabulary cards from each student's collection. They write sentences using just those words. Sampling is a reliable way to test, especially if you do it regularly.

> Online: Choose three words students have studied. Each student writes a sentence using each word in a document and sends their three sentences to you.

Introducing Total Physical Response: Learning Through Movement

Students need to understand before they can speak. With James Asher's TPR (Total Physical Response), students move their bodies before they say the words. Actions make the meaning clear and anchor it in memory. TPR appeals to visual, aural, and kinesthetic learners. It offers plenty of practice and also immediate feedback because students self-correct as they observe classmates and the teacher. It is an excellent way to introduce vocabulary and structures. It works well in large classes and is ideal for beginners. Who could ask for more?

TPR takes a bit of practice, but it's worth it. After using it just a few times, you'll see how effective it is! Students enjoy TPR. They feel like they are playing games, so motivation and attention are high.

How to Use TPR

1. Repeat each step several times until most students are doing it correctly without looking to see what classmates are doing.

2. Be sure that every student imitates your actions. Without the physical actions, the words won't mean much or stay in their memories.

6.2 CLASSIC TPR: THE BASIC STEPS

LEVEL: High Beginning – Advanced

AIMS: Improving vocabulary and grammar, listening for specific information, repeating steps in a sequence

MATERIALS: Find a TPR action sequence online or create your own with vocabulary or structures your students are learning. Here is an example:

- Where are my car keys?
- Oh, here they are!
- Unlock the car door.
- Get into the car and shut the door.
- Fasten the seat belt.
- Adjust the back and side mirrors.
- Release the hand brake.
- Start the car.
- Turn on some really good music.
- Drive to a place you've never been.
- Be surprised!

Procedure:

1. Students just observe: For each line, you speak and do the actions. Students watch and listen.
2. Students add actions: You speak and do the actions again while students do the actions silently.

Procedure (continued):

3. Students add speaking: You speak but DO NOT act while students speak and do the actions.
4. Coach two students as they demonstrate pair work. First A says the sequence while B does the actions. Then they switch.
5. Students work on their own: Pair students to practice in the same way.

> Online: Put a pair in each breakout room.

Notes:
- Some students may begin speaking while they do the actions as early as Step 2. Others won't speak so soon. This is OK. They are all learning, and they'll speak as soon as they're ready.
- If you want students to see the words for sight/sound correspondence, share them before Step 4 or earlier. You might dictate the sequence or write it on the board as students copy it down.
- Step 5 is the most important one. It's where most of the practice happens. Students should do it several times with one partner or with a series of different partners.

6.3 LET'S ACT IT OUT FIRST!

This active routine pre-teaches vocabulary and raises students' curiosity. The example below is a narrative, but it also works for factual content. It's a chance to get creative with all sorts of input! Acting is great fun, and the listening or reading that follows becomes a very satisfying experience!

LEVEL: Beginning – Advanced

AIMS: Pre-teaching vocabulary and content, role playing with new words

Procedure:

1. From a reading or listening passage, choose a few words that may be new to your students. Write these on the board. For example, you might write "princess," "important," "tiger," and "hungry."

2. Before the class reads or listens to the passage, coach them to act it out. Bring a volunteer up to the front. Say, for example, "Rosie, please stand here. You're the princess." Whisper her lines to her: Say, "I'm a princess! I'm important!" Rosie gets into character and repeats this, saying "I'm a princess! I'm important!"

> Online: Send a student a private message in the chat telling them what to do and say.

3. Now bring up another student: "Yusuf, you're a tiger. Please stand like this." Whisper his lines to him. Yousef crouches a bit, extends his claws, bares his teeth and growls, "I'm a tiger. I'm hungry."

> Online: Send another student a private message in the chat telling them what to do and say.

Procedure (continued):

4. Continue to build the action as you bring more students up to the front. As you direct them, students move and repeat your prompts, acting out the meaning of words they will read or listen to.

5. Students are now eager to read!

6.4 DISAPPEARING VOCABULARY LIST

This memorization activity is great for pronunciation and sight-sound correspondence. Whether or not students know the meanings yet, working with words in this way is very effective. Lots of repetition and lots of fun make the words easier to learn and more memorable.

LEVEL: Beginning – Advanced

AIM: Introducing new words

Procedure:

1. Write on the board a list of words. Chant the list a few times. Students just listen while you model pronunciation.

2. Students chant the list in unison with you a few times as you point to each word. Keep the pace brisk!

3. Erase one word, putting a mark where it was in the list. This time, you stay silent. Students chant the whole list again as you point quickly to each word (or place where a word was erased). If some students don't remember a missing word, repeat Step 2.

4. Continue chanting the list over and over with your students, erasing words one at a time until the list is completely gone. It's fun to jump around in the list rather than always going from top to bottom. Students have the list memorized now!

5. Finally, point to each marked space silently while the class chants the entire list.

6. Students dictate the list, spelling out each word as you or a student writes the list back up on the board.

> This activity works equally well in an online class with no adaptations.

<u>**STAGE 2: WORK WITH THE WORDS**</u>

6.5 HOW WELL DO I KNOW THESE WORDS?

Students identify for themselves where their new words are on the path between unknown and mastered. Students love to see their progress graphically as they move their words from left to right in their chart, helping classmates as they do this. It's useful at all three stages of learning words.

LEVEL: Beginning – Advanced

AIM: Self-assessing progress with new words

MATERIALS: A pencil for every student, erasers (which can be shared), and a short list of words to show students. Be sure there are some words they already know.

Procedure:

1. Each student makes a chart with the column headings below.

2. Dictate the words: Everyone writes them, top to bottom, in the first column.

3. Individual work: Ask "How well do you know these words?" Students write each word again under column A, B, C, or D in their charts. (If possible, they do this in pencil. Later they will move some words farther to the right, and it's better to erase than cross out.)

The chart below shows examples of where one student might place four words. (Your list might have more than four words, of course.)

WORDS	A. I don't know this word	B. I have seen this word before	C. I understand this word.	D. I use this word easily.
1. paradigm	*paradigm*			
2. fast				*fast*
3. summary		*summary*		
4. race			*race*	

4. In groups, students talk to classmates about their charts, teaching and learning from one another. As students understand a word better, they erase it and re-write it in a column farther to the right in their chart.

> Online: Put a few students in each breakout room.

Extension: Students can personalize their chart by putting in words of their own choice.

Adapted from *Finding Family*, University of Michigan Press. Natalie Hess, Laurel Pollard, and Rick Kappra

6.6 ASSOCIATIONS: THIS REMINDS ME OF THAT

Making personal associations is a powerful way to remember new words. It's creative and fun! Students can use it at all three levels of vocabulary learning.

LEVEL: Intermediate – Advanced

AIMS: Reviewing and improving recall of vocabulary, eliciting conversation

Procedure:

1. List on the board some words students have studied and an association prompt such as "what color...?"

2. Choose one word from the list. Demonstrate how to use associations for long-term memory of new words by giving a few examples of your own. If the word is resilient, you might say:

   - For me, resilient is rainbow-colored because it can change.
   - Resilient reminds me of my aunt because she has had a hard life but always has a positive attitude.
   - Resilient reminds me of my grandfather, who had to move because of war. He made a new life.

3. In pairs or small groups, students tell one another about their own associations with each of the words on the board.

   > Online: Put a pair or a few students in each breakout room.

4. As a class, volunteers tell some of their associations.

   > Online: Students return to the main room before sharing.

5. To anchor the words in memory, students add their association notes to their vocabulary cards.

6. There's no need to stop with colors! Students can associate new words with a person, a time of day, or a place, for example. They may have their own ideas for associations. Be imaginative!

 This works well after "Vocabulary Cards" (Activity 6.1).

6.7 ASSOCIATIONS: VOCABULARY HOUSE

This ongoing association activity is a powerful way to "anchor" words in memory. Students keep their Vocabulary House throughout your course, adding new words and sharing their "house" in class from time to time.

A wonderful side effect: when students tell one another why they put each new word in a particular room, they learn a lot about one another!

LEVEL: Beginning – Advanced

AIMS: Forming personal associations with words, telling personal stories, eliciting conversation

MATERIALS: Extra-large sheets of paper, one per student

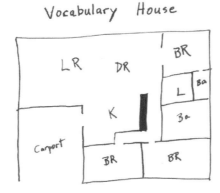

Procedure:

Demonstration

1. On one section of the board, list some words students have studied.

2. On a large section of the board, draw a simple floor plan of a place you have lived. As you draw, tell students, "This is my vocabulary house."

3. Name the spaces you're drawing: "This is the kitchen." Put a K in that space. "This is the yard." Put a Y there. "This is the garden." Label it with a G.

4. Point out that your rooms are empty: they have no furniture and are large enough to hold plenty of words.

5. Demonstrate how associations work. Tell the class, "I'm going to write new words in my rooms." Students pick any word from the board and challenge you to put it in your vocabulary house. Write it in one of your rooms and tell them why you made this association, e.g,

   • "I'm writing 'forbidden' in my bedroom because my mom never let me play computer games until my homework was done."

   • "I'm putting 'giraffe' in the yard because there's a big tree there, and I can imagine a giraffe eating the top leaves."

   • "I'll put 'clean' in the kitchen because I used to wash my hands at the sink there."

   • "I'm writing 'orbit' where the TV would be because I saw a show about space exploration."

Note: This can take a bit of creative thinking. That's the point! The effort of making an association plants deep roots in the brain.

Procedure (continued):

Individual Work

6. Students choose a home where they have many memories and draw their own floor plan.

7. Students select a word from the board, associate it with a place in their vocabulary house, and write the word in that room. They do this with several words.

Pair or Small Group Work

8. Students tell each other why they put each word where they did. Some associations may be personal, so teach students that they can tell each other, "I'd rather not say."

> Online: Put two or three students in each breakout room.

9. They keep their vocabulary house, adding words to it and explaining their associations to classmates throughout the course.

6.8 WORDS I NEED TO REVIEW

Why spend time choosing words you think students need to review? They know better than you do! This quick routine invites students to guide you to the words they want to review before you launch your planned vocabulary activity. It's useful at all three stages of learning words.

LEVEL: Beginning – Advanced
AIM: Finding words students want to review

Procedure:

1. On a regular basis, post on the board words your students have recently studied. Students come up and put a check mark by words they want to review.

> Online: Launch a survey where students can indicate the words they don't remember. If you want the class to see which words were chosen most, share the results of the survey.

2. Choose the words with the most check marks. You have options here:

   • If you have time, invite students to mingle, asking classmates for help. Students are often the best teachers! Circulate, helping as needed.

   > Online: Put a pair or trio in each breakout room.

   • If your time is limited, re-teach selected words yourself.

3. Go on to your planned vocabulary activity, focusing on the words that need reviewing most.

STAGE 3: MAKE THE WORDS MY OWN

6.9 ASSOCIATIONS: PERSONAL SENTENCES

People remember new words much better when they write personal sentences drawing on their own knowledge and experiences

LEVEL: High Beginning – Advanced

AIM: Anchoring new words/phrases in memory

Procedure:

1. Individually, students write a list of words or phrases/idioms they understand but are not yet using freely.

2. In small groups, students help one another write personal sentences for each of their words/phrases. For example, if the word is "book," a student might write, "I bring my book to school." For "frustrated," a student might write, "I feel frustrated when_____."

> Online: Put a few students in each breakout room.

3. Circulate, offering help when students ask for assistance.

4. Volunteers share some of their sentences proudly.

> Online: Students return to the main room before sharing.

6.10 TWO-IN-ONE VOCABULARY REVIEW

This association game activates students' imaginations by challenging them to create meaningful contexts for words that don't seem to be related to each other. It's challenging to use two unrelated words in the same sentence, and the challenge makes both words more memorable!

LEVEL: Intermediate – Advanced

AIMS: Reviewing vocabulary, improving fluency, helping classmates

Procedure:

1. With your students, write on the board a list of words to be reviewed.

2. Circle two unrelated words on the board. In pairs, students quickly talk together and create a sentence that makes the meaning of both words clear. Tell them you might call on either of them, so their job is to make sure their partner is ready to speak.

> Online: Put a pair in each breakout room.

Procedure (continued):

3. When both partners are prepared, they raise their hands together.

> Online: Students return to the main room when they are ready.

4. Choose a pair and call on one of them to say their sentence to the whole class. Other pairs listen carefully and decide whether the speaker used the two words in a way that makes both meanings clear. If the sentence is incorrect or doesn't make both meanings clear, other students may make suggestions.

Notes:

a. This can be challenging; keep the standards high! Simply including a word is not enough; the sentence has to provide enough context to make the meaning clear.

b. Encourage partners to take responsibility for helping each other. If you call on Roberto and he isn't able to produce a sentence immediately, pause the game. You might say kindly, "Ah, Roberto and Kamran forgot to help each other say their sentence out loud. Let's all get back in pairs and practice." Pairs who were prepared have to practice again. This doesn't take long, and the gentle peer pressure activates everyone. Students quickly learn to talk and listen fast in their pairs to get each other ready.

5. Repeat the activity, circling two new unrelated words. Continue as long as there is interest.

Variation: More advanced students may work alone to make a sentence with two unrelated words, then compare their sentences with others.

6.11 POEMS FOR STUDENTS BY STUDENTS

This activity helps students write poems about one another. Use it later in a course when students know one another well. You'll all enjoy the bloom of goodwill!

LEVEL: Intermediate – Advanced

AIMS: Writing to describe people, expanding vocabulary, building classroom community

Procedure:

Demonstration

1. Tell your students they will be writing a poem about a classmate.

2. Demonstrate by using yourself. Students enjoy learning about their teacher! For example, write "Laurel Lynn" on the board. This becomes the first line of a poem your students will write.

3. For the second line of your demonstration poem, elicit adjectives that describe you. With your class, write three of these under your name. Examples: funny, kind, creative.

Procedure (continued):

4. For the third line of your poem, elicit "-ing" verb phrases from your class. Together, choose three of these and write them on the board. Examples: planning our classes, laughing with us, helping us learn from our mistakes.

5. For the fourth line of your poem, elicit short sentences that describe you and with your class choose one appropriate sentence. Example: "She cares about us."

6. Add the last name, in this case "Pollard," as the final line of the poem.

7. The poem on the board now reads:

    "Laurel Lynn

    Funny, kind, creative

    Planning our classes, laughing with us, helping us learn from our mistakes

    She cares about us

    Pollard"

Students Write their Poems

8. Give each student the name of a randomly selected classmate to write a poem about. Important: Tell students their poems must reflect only positive qualities of their classmates.

9. Give students some time to write their poems. Early finishers may pair up to refine their work.

    > Online: Students use the raised-hand icon when they finish writing. Put early finishers in pairs in breakout rooms.

10. Volunteers read their poems aloud.

    > Online: Students return to the main room before sharing.

11. Students give their poems to the classmate they wrote about.

6.12 GETTING REAL WITH OUR NEW WORDS

Students identify for themselves the new words they're confident with. They use them in real contexts outside the classroom and report back on their experiences.

LEVEL: Beginning – Advanced

AIM: Using new words in real contexts to anchor them in memory

Procedure:

1. Students look over words they've learned and write down three they think are the most useful.

2. In groups of 3 or 4, students talk about their words, explaining how they have used these words – or will use them – outside class.

> Online: Put a few students in each breakout room.

3. In a later class, they share their experiences with these words in class.

6.13 TWO UNRELATED PICTURES

In this activity, students discover the similarities between two seemingly unrelated pictures. They enjoy their classmates' creativity and surprise themselves with the associations they make.

LEVEL: Intermediate – Advanced

AIMS: Discussing similarities, generating new vocabulary

MATERIALS: Four interesting unrelated pictures large enough for the whole class to see

Procedure:

1. To demonstrate the activity, hold up two pictures that seem completely unrelated to each other and ask the class, "How are these two pictures related? What is similar between them?" Be patient. If necessary, start by saying, "Well, they're both printed on paper!" to reassure students that you're not looking for a particular "right" answer. Students will soon offer their own ideas.

> Online: Share your screen to show the pictures.

2. Display the pictures where everyone can see them. Put students in pairs.

> Online: Put a pair in each breakout room.

3. Partners look at the pictures, asking, "How are these two pictures related?". They come up with as many ideas as they can while one of them takes notes.

Procedure (continued):

4. As a class, volunteers tell how these very different pictures are related. If time allows, classmates may offer more ideas about these two pictures.

    Online: Students return to the main room.

5. After each pair presents, lead a round of applause for their creativity.

6. If time allows, repeat the activity with your other two pictures.

Extension for Vocabulary: As each pair presents, write on the board useful words and phrases that come up. Ask whether these are new words for some students and practice them.

Variation: In another lesson, bring pairs of similar pictures. Students can play "How Are These Different?"

Chapter Seven

Grammar

Grammar is the glue that holds language together. It helps us decide who bit whom and when in the sentence, "The dog bit a man." It helps us understand who is to treat whom and how in the sentence, "Be good to yourself." The activities in this chapter will help you introduce, practice, and reinforce grammatical patterns with your students.

7.1 SENTENCE CONTRACTION

This simple activity helps students understand sentence structure by finding the "skeleton" of a sentence. There is usually more than one way to trim a sentence down to its basic elements. In the process, students learn a lot about grammar and punctuation!

LEVEL: Intermediate – Advanced

AIMS: Understanding grammatical structures, identifying the main clause in a sentence

Procedure:

1. Put a long sentence on the board. For example, in an advanced class, you might write, "My grandmother, who lived in New York, smoked an expensive little cigar every afternoon of her life, but in spite of this dangerous habit, lived to be eighty-six years old."

2. Ask students, "What can we remove and still have a correct sentence?"

3. Each time a student calls out a suggestion, put parentheses around that word or phrase.

4. The class reads aloud what is left (omitting what is in parentheses) and decides whether this is still a grammatically possible sentence.

5. If that deletion works, erase what is in parentheses.

6. Continue the procedure, calling on students until the sentence is as simple as it can be. Feel free to change words a bit to get down to the absolute "skeleton" of the sentence. For example, your class might end with, "My grandmother smoked cigars but lived to be old."

> This activity works equally well in an online class with no adaptations.

7.2 SENTENCE EXPANSION

This exercise helps students write more interesting sentences. It's also a very effective way to practice many grammatical structures.

LEVEL: Intermediate – Advanced

AIMS: Adding details to writing, practicing structures

Procedure:

1. Put a simple sentence on the board, for example, "Salem does homework." Leave plenty of space between the words.

2. Ask students what they can add to this sentence. You may accept all offerings, or you may ask for particular structures.

3. Students who want to add something say the whole sentence, including their addition. For example, one student may say, "sometimes." The class chorally repeats the now-longer sentence: "Salem sometimes does homework." If the next student suggests "in the middle of the night," the class says, "Salem sometimes does homework in the middle of the night."

Procedure (continued):

4. With each addition, ask the class whether it is still grammatically possible. If it is, write the new addition in the sentence or invite a student to do this. This step is the heart of the activity: the class explores what can and cannot be done with a sentence.

5. Continue the activity, accepting contributions until the sentence is stretched to ridiculous lengths. If students run out of ideas too soon, offer prompts such as Where? When? Why? How? How many? How much? What kind of? How often? Who else? What else?

> This activity works equally well in an online class with no adaptations.

7.3 SUBSTITUTION DRILLS

Use this classic drill to practice any grammar at any level. Students have to think fast, which is fun! Substitution drills take a bit of practice at first, but once you and your students find your rhythm, you will want to use them again and again!

LEVEL: Beginning – Advanced

AIM: Practicing grammar holistically

MATERIALS: Write a list of cues you will use to give your class practice with structures they've been learning. (See the example notes under "Teacher" in the table below.)

Procedure:

1. Dictate a sentence. The class repeats it chorally.

2. Dictate one change at a time. The class says the revised sentence. (Note: If some students are getting it wrong, just gesture for the whole class to say it again. As they listen to one another, more and more students will be saying the correctly revised sentence.)

It's easy to adapt substitution drills for different levels:
For beginners, you might change one element at a time.

Teacher	Class
Yoshiko got up at 7:00.	Yoshiko got up at 7:00.
8:00	Yoshiko got up at **8:00.**
Marco	**Marco** got up at 8:00.
(Continue with several more changes.)	(The class says the revised sentences.)

Procedure (continued):

In an intermediate class, you might change an element that requires the students to make more than one change in the sentence.

Teacher	Class
Maria drives her car to school.	Maria drives her car to school.
Ali	**Ali** drives **his** car to school.
Abdu and Abeke	**Abdu and Abeke drive their** car to school.
grocery store	Abdu and Abeke drive their car to **the grocery store**
(Continue with several more changes.)	(The class says the revised sentences.)

In an advanced class, mix it up however you like!

Teacher	Class
Yesterday I saw a horse in the park.	Yesterday I saw a horse in the park.
every day	**Every day** I **see** a horse in the park.
pool	Every day I see a horse in the **pool.**
two	Every day I see **two horses** in the pool.
why	**Why do** I see two horses in the pool?
elephants	Why do I see two **elephants** in the pool?
(Continue with several more changes.)	(The class says the revised sentences.)

Note: This can get very funny! Continue as long as there is interest.

This activity works equally well in an online class with no adaptations.

7.4 STORY CHAINS

In this activity, students take the second half of a sentence and use it as the first half of a new sentence. It's creative, fun, and useful for practicing many grammatical structures. The example below, using "if" clauses, is just one structure you can practice with a Story Chain. Try it with adverbial clauses or other structures that deal with time sequences or cause and effect!

LEVEL: Intermediate – Advanced
AIMS: Practicing structures that deal with time sequences or cause and effect

Procedure:

1. If you are practicing "if" clauses, write on the board a sentence frame like this: "If I _____, I will_____. Say a sentence such as "If I make a million dollars, I will travel around the world."

2. In pairs or small groups, students create a new sentence starting with the second half of the one you just said. For example, "If I travel around the world, I will stop in Rome." Each group raises their hands together when all of them are ready to say their new sentence.

Procedure (continued):

> Online: Every student works independently to make a new sentence. Students use the raised-hand icon when they are ready to say their new sentence.

3. When everyone is prepared to speak, call on one student. The class repeats this sentence chorally.

4. The groups go back to work, repeating steps 2 and 3: everyone produces a new sentence, the groups choose one to present, and the class repeats it to continue the story chain, e.g., "If I stop in Rome, I will learn Italian." "If learn Italian, I will make new friends." A better example: . . . "I may fall in love."

> Online: Again, students work independently.

5. Continue as long as interest is high. These story chains often go in unexpected directions!

Supercharge Your Teaching!

For powerful ways to talk less while students practice more during class, see "Quick Pair-Share" and "Numbered Heads Together" in our free guide *Supercharge Your Teaching*, downloadable from ProLinguaLearning.com.

7.5 PREPOSITION HOUSE

Students play with prepositions of place or time by imagining where a mouse may be hiding. The example below, using prepositions of place, will get you started. Students' personal sketches make the associations memorable!

LEVEL: Beginning – Advanced
AIMS: Reviewing prepositions of place, reviewing furnishings in a house
MATERIALS: A list of prepositions of place

Procedure:

1. Ask students to imagine they saw a mouse in their house, and they don't know where it went.

2. Share a list of prepositions of place.

3. Put a few sentence frames on the board, for example:

   - "It might be ___ the ___."
   - "Maybe it's ____ the ___."
   - "I think it went _____ the ____."

4. Each student sketches a floor plan of a place they know well, including some furnishings and closets.

Procedure (continued):

5. Time for some fun! In pairs, students take turns talking as they write prepositions in their sketch. For example, a student might write the word "under" below their bed, telling their partner, "It might be under the bed."

> Online: Put a pair in each breakout room.

6. They continue writing prepositions in their sketch and talking to each other using sentence frames like the ones you posted.

7. As a class, volunteers share the silliest sentences they came up with.

> Online: Students return to the main room before sharing.

Extension for prepositions of time: Post a list of prepositions of time and ask students when they saw the mouse. In pairs, they take turns saying sentences such as

- "I saw it under the bed at 8:00."
- "I saw it behind the kitchen door before breakfast."
- "I think it came under the door during my shower."

7.6 CONJUNCTION CARDS

This activity is useful for practicing coordinating conjunctions and negative forms.

LEVEL: Intermediate – Advanced
AIMS: Using conjunctions and negative forms
MATERIALS: Blank index cards

Procedure:

1. Choose a conjunction from this list: and, but, or, nor, so, for, yet.

2. Give a few examples on the board of one conjunction joining parts of sentences. For example, if you have chosen 'but', write:

I like coffee,	but	I don't like tea.
Toshi has a motorcycle,	but	he doesn't have a car.
London is foggy,	but	it isn't a bad place to live.

3. As a class, invite volunteers to contribute a few more examples for the conjunction you have chosen.

4. Students create three pairs of short sentences that could be joined by the conjunction. For example, to practice "but," students would make six cards that might look like this:

Procedure (continued):

Hee Jin doesn't study.	She does well on all her tests.
I like ice cream.	Apples are better for me.
Ernesto is a good student.	He doesn't talk much in class.

> Online: Students write their sentences on a document that can be shared. Before they share it with a classmate, they should mix up their sentences in the document.

5. Students mix up their six cards and exchange sets of cards with classmates.

> Online: Put a pair in each breakout room.

6. Students re-match the mixed-up cards they have received. They show these to the originating student to confirm they've matched the cards correctly. They write the complete sentences, adding a comma and the conjunction.

> Online: Students return to the main room and read their document to the class.

Variation: With more advanced classes, add challenge by using not one, but two or three conjunctions at a time. If you write on the board, for example, "or," "so," "because," student pairs might produce these six cards:

Reina does her homework.	She watches TV.
I can't find my keys.	I can't drive.
I hate coffee.	It keeps me awake at night.

Note: When students have different opinions about how to re-match the sentences and which conjunctions to use, you have created a genuine speaking opportunity!

7.7 NUMBERS IN MY LIFE

Students enjoy the guessing-game aspect of this activity. They practice information questions, learn a little bit about you and their classmates, and get practice saying numbers in the target language.

LEVEL: Intermediate – Advanced

AIMS: Practicing questions, improving numeracy in the target language

Procedure:

1. Write on the board five or six numbers in your life – for example, your shoe size, your age, the numbers in your street address, your zip code, the number of children you have, or your favorite number.

2. Students ask you questions, trying to elicit what the numbers refer to. For example, "How old are you?"

3. After students have guessed as many numbers as they can, teach the rest. For example, "This number is my street address."

4. Once the students know what your numbers refer to, they form small groups and write down three of their own "secret numbers." They guess what their classmates' numbers are about, and then ask each other questions to find out.

> Online: Put a few students in each breakout room.

5. Volunteers tell something interesting they learned about a classmate.

> Online: Students return to the main session before sharing.

7.8 TRUTH, TRUTH, LIE

Students tell two truths and one lie about themselves in this game. It elicits genuine questions and encourages careful listening. Students get creative about the lies they tell!

LEVEL: Intermediate – Advanced

AIMS: Practicing correct formation of questions, getting to know classmates

Procedure:

1. Write on the board three statements about yourself. Tell students that two statements are true and one is a lie. For example:

    • "I used to live in Cairo, Egypt."

    • "I know how to fly an airplane."

    • "I have six brothers and sisters."

2. Every student writes three questions designed to find out more about your statements. For example:

    • "Where did you live in Cairo?"

    • "What kind of airplane can you fly?"

    • "How old are all of your brothers and sisters?"

3. In pairs or small groups, classmates check to see that their questions are grammatically correct. Circulate, putting a checkmark by correctly formed questions.

> Online: Put a pair or small group in each breakout room. Visit the rooms and check questions using the chat. Have students send you numbered questions, and you can tell them which are correct.

Procedure (continued):

4. Call on students quickly to ask you their questions. Students take notes about your answers. If someone says an incorrectly formed question, smile but don't answer it. They may revise it themselves or ask a classmate for help.

> Online: Students return to the main room for this step.

5. Any student who catches you in a suspicious answer may challenge you. Teach the phrase "I know what the lie is!"

6. If the student has discovered your lie and can explain why, confess and declare them the winner.

7. Now students get to play! Everyone writes three statements about themselves. Use these as the basis for further rounds of the game.

7.9 BINGO

Bingo offers a game-like format to liven up repeated practice of structures or vocabulary. Students discover that they have to listen carefully in order to win.

LEVEL: Beginning – Advanced
AIMS: Reviewing grammar and vocabulary, listening for specific information

Procedure:

1. Draw a 9- or 16-square grid on the board.

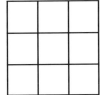

2. Every student copies the grid onto a paper.

3. Ask students, "What are some words we want to review?" With their help, create a list of words on the board. This will become the basis for a grammar lesson. Do not write the words in the grid you have made.

4. Each student writes 9 (or 16) of the words in their grids in random order. Every grid will have the words in a different arrangement.

5. Now the grammar practice begins! Choose one task for your lesson and call on a few students to model the task. On different days, you might have students:

   • ask a question using the word.

   • say a negative sentence using the word.

   • say a sentence using the word and also using a conjunction or a preposition you have written on the board.

   • say a sentence using a particular verb tense you have written on the board.

Procedure (continued):

6. Call out the words one at a time. As students find a word in their grid, they cross it off.

7. As soon as any student has a vertical, horizontal, or diagonal straight line of crossed-out words, they call out, "Bingo!" Challenge this lucky student to perform the assigned task correctly for all the words in their "Bingo" row. If they can do this, declare them the winner! If they cannot, continue the game until another student calls "Bingo!" and performs all of the tasks correctly. This stage of the game is GREAT for accountability and memory.

Variation: If you are reviewing vocabulary, students play Bingo by saying a sentence using the word correctly.

Note: To liven up a quiz, play Bingo and ask students to write their sentences. Then collect the papers.

> This activity works equally well in an online class with no adaptations.

7.10 WHO AM I?

Students have fun learning about classmates as they practice yes/no questions. Use this at the beginning of a new course. Because you will be adding your own information to the game, students will also have a chance to learn about you!

LEVEL: Intermediate – Advanced

AIMS: Practicing yes/no questions, getting to know classmates, generating conversation

SETUP: For online classes, create a shared document that includes three blank lines per student. Number the lines so that students know where to type.

Procedure:

1. All at the same time, you and your students write on the board three facts about yourselves in three different places: name, country of origin, and something interesting that few people know about. If you don't have enough board space, people can post on the walls a separate note for each fact.

> Online: Direct students to the shared document that you have posted in an application or program such as Microsoft Teams or Google Drive, which will allow everyone to see each other's facts instantly/synchronously. All students write each of their three facts on the same document on a blank line where no one has written yet.

2. Everyone takes a moment to read this mixed-up mass of information.

3. Each student lists on a piece of paper your name and their classmates' names.

4. The mingle begins! Students approach one classmate at a time and ask yes/no questions about the facts that were posted. For example, "Are you from Senegal?" "Do you know how to fly a plane?" When a classmate says, 'Yes!', they write this fact next to that classmate's name on their list.

Procedure (continued):

> Online: Put small groups in each breakout room. Students question one another and start filling in their papers. After a short time, shuffle the breakout rooms. Students ask more questions and continue completing their papers. Circulate among the breakout rooms so students can ask about your facts.

5. In pairs or small groups, students may talk with one another about what they learned. (e.g., Edith is from Ecuador and can repair bicycles.)

> Online: Shuffle the breakout rooms again for this conversation.

6. With the whole class, volunteers tell something they learned and why this particularly interested them.

> Online: Students return to the main room before sharing.

7.11 PERSONAL QUESTIONS

In this activity, students generate information questions, then use them to get acquainted.

LEVEL: Intermediate – Advanced
AIMS: Practicing question formation, getting acquainted, eliciting conversation
MATERIALS: A small container

Procedure:

1. Say, "We're going to make up interesting questions to ask each other." For example:
    *   Who is your best friend? Tell me about them.
    *   Did you ever lose anything important? What happened?
    *   What is something good that happened to you recently?
    *   What would you like to be doing five years from now?

2. Students write more questions. They bring their questions to you before putting them into the box. You may:
    *   point out errors and ask the writer to correct them
    *   direct the writer to a classmate for help
    *   correct errors yourself
    *   allow students who finish early to write an extra question

> Online: Students send you their questions in the chat. If the questions are clear and correct, post them on a shared screen. If not, offer corrections.

Procedure (continued):

3. Once you have a few more questions in the container than there are students, the activity begins. Each student picks a question slip from the container. Everyone circulates with their question, approaching one classmate and having short conversations about their two question slips. Note: Teach students the phrase "I'd rather not say" for questions they don't want to answer.

> Online: Ask students to choose two questions each from the shared list. Put a pair in each breakout room to have a short conversation about one of the questions.

4. After students use their question one time, they come back to the container, redeposit that question, take a different question slip, and find a different partner to talk with.

> Online: After a short time, shuffle the breakout rooms. Students discuss the second question they chose. If their partner chooses a question they have already discussed, they may return to the main room to pick a different question.

5. Continue as long as there is interest.

6. As a class, volunteers tell something interesting they learned about a classmate.

> Online: Students return to the main room before sharing.

Variation: You may dictate or develop with your class a set of questions to target a particular grammar point. For example, the questions may require a verb tense you have studied. If a partner makes an error during Steps 3 and 4, encourage students to say, "Try again!"

7.12 FROM PICTURE TO STORIES: PAST, PRESENT, AND FUTURE

With a picture to spark imagination, students use all the verb tenses they know to create original stories. Their stories can range from tragic to comic to ridiculous, giving everyone a chance to play with their new language.

LEVEL: Intermediate – Advanced
AIMS: Practicing verb tenses
MATERIALS: An interesting picture large enough for your class to see

Procedure:

1. Show an interesting picture. Give students time to really look at it.

2. With your class, discuss and write on the board any new words students may need in order to make up stories about the picture.

3. Individually, students write three sentences suggested by the picture, one about the past, another about the present, and a third about the future.

Procedure (continued):

4. Story time! In pairs, students create a story using their sentences or other ideas that occur to them. If you want everyone to tell a story, give your students time to practice what they will say. If you want everyone to write a story, give them time to write. Encourage them to use their imaginations!

> Online: Put a pair in each breakout room.

5. To share their stories, students may tell them to the whole class and/or post their written stories for others to read. As they do, take advantage of the opportunities to welcome 'interlanguage' errors as you explore together what's possible in the target language.

> Online: Students return to the main room before sharing.

Extension: Invite your more advanced students to add modal auxiliaries and more verb tenses to the mix. You might be surprised by the sentences they made / might make / are making / will have made / will have been trying to make . . . in short, this can turn into a wild exploration of language and ideas.

INDEXES OF ACTIVITY FUNCTIONS/TOPICS

1. BEGINNING-LEVEL ACTIVITIES

These activities work equally well for high beginners and more advanced students. For an entire book of low-level activities, please see our companion book, *Zero Prep for Beginners*.

2. COMMUNITY-BUILDING ACTIVITIES

These activities help students to know classmates better.

3. CONVERSATION STRATEGIES

These activities include expressions for specific communication needs such as interrupting politely, offering corrections, declining to answer, etc.

4. DISCUSSION STARTERS

These activities spark lively conversation.

5. ENERGIZERS

These activities lift the energy level of a class.

6. FLUENCY-BUILDING ACTIVITIES

In these activities, the aim is quantity: students listen, speak, read, or write without stopping. Inhibition lessens and confidence grows!

7. IN-READING ACTIVITIES

We know about pre-reading and post-reading activities. Here are two great activities that activate students' skills while they are reading.

8. MULTIPLE INTELLIGENCES

These activities engage "intelligences" other than the strictly verbal, including artistic, musical, kinesthetic, spatial, and emotional intelligences.

9. OUTSIDE THE CLASSROOM

These activities use the community beyond the classroom.

10. PREVIEWING OR REVIEWING CLASS MATERIAL

These activities work well as introductions to new material or as practice tasks for previously learned material.

11. PRONUNCIATION

Many of the activities in this book can be used to focus on pronunciation; the following have pronunciation as a primary focus.

12. REPEATABLE ACTIVITIES TO USE THROUGHOUT A COURSE

Here's a sampling of activities that many teachers use again and again throughout their courses.

13. SETTLING-DOWN ACTIVITIES

When energy is high, these activities help a class quiet down.

14. SHORT ACTIVITIES

These activities can be done briefly if you have only a little extra time in your lesson.

15. STUDENTS HELPING STUDENTS

In these activities, classmates give and receive help from one another.

ALPHABETICAL INDEX OF ACTIVITIES